Vygotsky in Action in the Early Years
The 'Key to Learning' curriculum

Do you want to prepare the children in your class for the educational challenges they will face in the years to come?

Do you recognise the value of strong foundations for learning but wonder how to implement these in your setting?

Vygotsky in Action in the Early Years is based on the concepts of Lev Vygotsky, one of the twentieth century's most influential theorists in the field of early years education. Drawing upon the 'Key to Learning' curriculum, a unique and inspiring programme of cognitive development activities for the Foundation Stage and Key Stage 1, the author shows how you can encourage young children to become independent learners.

Vygotsky in Action in the Early Years transforms Vygotsky's theory of child development into clear, accessible activities for children between the ages of three and seven, and explains the theory underpinning the practice, enabling practitioners to apply it in their own setting.

This invaluable resource includes examples of ready-to-use activities from a total of over 600 specially designed learning experiences, in 12 teacher-friendly curriculum modules. With links to the Early Years Foundation Stage learning goals, this comprehensive programme helps you enable children to:

- plan and organise their own activities, through a balance of teacher-directed and child-initiated activities;
- openly express their point of view, developing language, listening and attention skills;
- solve problems creatively, using thinking skills;
- interact freely and confidently with others, improving social skills;
- become self-confident, self-motivated learners, with the mindset and mental tools they need for later learning securely in place.

Early years practitioners and Key Stage 1 teachers wanting to extend and enrich children's cognitive development will find this an invaluable tool to complement and systemise existing good practice.

Galina Dolya is the Curriculum Director of 'Key to Learning' and a renowned world expert on the practical application of Vygotsky's Theory of Learning and Development.

Routledge
Taylor & Francis Group
LONDON AND NEW YORK

First published in Great Britain by GDH Publishing in 2007
This version published 2010
by Routledge
2 Park Square, Milton Park, Abingdon, Oxon OX14 4RN

Simultaneously published in the USA and Canada
by Routledge
711 Third Avenue, New York, NY 10017

Routledge is an imprint of the Taylor & Francis Group, an informa business

Editor: Judy Holder
Art Direction and Design: David Higgins
Layout and Typesetting: Anna Tkachenko, Anthology Pbl., St Petersburg, Russia
Illustrations for Story Grammar: Elena Kiss
Photography: Tony Hardacre, Andy Sewell, Christy Dolya and GDH Publishing
Clip-art credit: Serif
Printed and bound in Great Britain

British Library Cataloguing in Publication Data
A catalogue record for this book is available from the British Library

Library of Congress Cataloging in Publication Data
Dolya, Galina.
  Vygotsky in action in the early years : the key to learning curriculum /
Galina Dolya.
    p. cm.
  Includes bibliographical references.
1. Learning, Psychology of. 2. Early childhood education. 3. Vygotskii, L.
S. (Lev Semenovich), 1896-1934. I. Title.
  LB1060.D59 2010
  370.15–dc22

                                                                    2009018314

ISBN10: 0-415-55229-X (pbk)
ISBN10: 0-203-86481-6 (ebk)

ISBN13: 978-0-415-55229-5 (pbk)
ISBN13: 978-0-203-86481-4 (ebk)

CONTENTS

DEDICATION

To all our grandchildren, Catherine, Deniska, Alexander, Leo, Jos, Seryozha, Olivia, Josh and Aaron.

To Olga Dyachenko, my inspiration, mentor and sadly missed friend.

To Leonid Venger, the unsung hero of Early Childhood Education.

ACKNOWLEDGEMENTS

Many people have contributed to this book. My special thanks and sincere gratitude go to:

The prominent Russian researchers, psychologists and educationalists from the Vygotskian school who created the ideas which are the foundation of the Key to Learning Curriculum: Leonid Venger, Olga Dyachenko, Nikolai Veraksa, Alexander Venger, Irina Burlakova, Natalya Denisenkova, Elena Gorshkova, Valentina Kholmovskaya, Tatiana Lavrentieva, Lidia Pavlova, Yuri Pavlov and Galina Uradovskyh.

Nikolai Veraksa, my teacher and co-author with whom I had lengthy and invaluable discussions, for providing a rich source of material, expertise and insight.

Judy Holder, my editor, whose commentary, suggestions, sustained help, invaluable input and patient editing added much more clarity to the text.

Sue Palmer and Madeleine Portwood for their professional support and for taking time from their busy schedules to read and review the work.

The professionals in this field who have given me constant encouragement and feedback during the whole period of the development of the Key to Learning curriculum: Alex Kozulin, Sir Christopher Ball, Kathy Sylva, Ruth Kaufmann, Lois Holzman, Claire and David Mills.

The many people who in many different ways have given added value to the work: Scott Goodson, Maciek and Ida Winiarek, Anthology Publishing, Nicola Tuffnell, Paul Higgins, Larisa Dolya, Alexander Veraksa, Fiona Boyle, Chris Higgins, Jill Johnson, Vicky Parsey, Nancy Oxenham, Meg Thompson, Hayley Lakin, Libby Hartman, Tracy Wilson, Elizabeth Hunter, the teachers and children of Applecroft Primary School, William Reynolds Infants School, Lumley Nursery and Infants School and the Chelsea Group of Children Teaching Centre whose feedback has been invaluable in completing this book.

All the teachers and children who are implementing the Key to Learning curriculum and who constantly surprise me with their creative and innovative use of the programmes.

To Anna Tkachenko, Anna Nekludova, Yuri Mednikov for their creative book design, typesetting and especially for their patience and positive attitude in dealing with last minute changes.

Last but not least to David, my husband and colleague, without whose computer design, encouragement and emotional support each day, this book would never have been possible.

The human being is a possibility

Merab Mamardashvili

FOREWORD

Key to Learning is phenomenally impressive. It has depth and breadth, rigour and flexibility, insight and inclusion. It truly is a Vygotskian approach, carrying through to the 21st century his monumental discovery that human learning and development are a unified whole.

Unlike any other curriculum I am aware of, *Key to Learning* relates to young children as, in Vygotsky's words, 'a head taller than they are' – which is an essential characteristic of a developmental learning environment.

Lois Holzman, Developmental Psychologist, writer, Director of East Side Institute, New York

Several decades of research by Vygotskian scholars in Russia had led to the development of *Key to Learning* prototype. Now this curriculum is available in English and attuned to the needs of children of the 21st century. It accomplishes probably one of the most difficult tasks in the field of early education – preparing children for rigorous formal education and at the same time fostering their age-specific behaviour and creativity.

Professor Alex Kozulin, author of 'Vygotsky's Psychology: A Biography of Ideas' and 'Psychological Tools: A Socio-cultural Approach to Education'

As a primary teacher, I've been hooked on the work of Lev Vygotsky since first discovering his writing in the 1980s. His theory that human beings have created a set of 'cultural tools' which can be passed on through the generations is both intellectually powerful and professionally empowering.

What's more, the Vygotskian pedagogical model – scaffolding children's learning within their 'Zone of Proximal Development' – provides a truly developmental approach, and his stress on 'unlocking possibilities' within children's minds is a much more exciting and liberating vision of education than our western preoccupation with measuring current progress against arbitrary standards.

In *Key to Learning* Galina Dolya transforms all this Vygotskian theory into a clear, accessible course of practice for children between the ages of three and seven. Through two small-group sessions a day – as part of a language rich, play-based early years curriculum – the twelve strands of the Developmental Cognitive Curriculum provide them with a basic toolkit to develop learning abilities and enable them to access all areas of human knowledge.

As school systems throughout the UK become increasingly aware of the importance of structured age-appropriate practice for the under sevens, I hope *Key to Learning* will prove the key that helps a generation of British teachers to discover the excitement and effectiveness of Vygotskian principles and practice.

Sue Palmer, writer, broadcaster and consultant on education of young children

For two years I have evaluated the effect of the *Key to Learning* Developmental Cognitive Curriculum on a group of young learners in County Durham. Their progress across a range of skills, but particularly in the area of language and communication is remarkable. In my forty years of research in education, I have never seen a programme which develops language and communication as effectively as *Key to Learning* does.

What is striking about *Key to Learning* is its inclusivity. Children who previously struggled to acquire new skills, enjoyed their activities as much as the more able. Boys and girls were equally engaged as their imagination flourished. Clearly *Key to Learning* has a marked impact on the child's cognitive development.

Key to Learning crosses cultural boundaries and I would recommend that any teacher involved with children in the Early Years should read this book and if possible visit a setting that is using this curriculum. The experience will be unforgettable.

Dr Madeleine Portwood, Specialist Senior Educational Psychologist, Durham LEA

LEV VYGOTSKY – A THINKER WHO CHANGED TEACHING

There is nothing so practical as a good theory.

Kurt Lewin

What is the secret of the vitality of Vygotskian ideas? What is so special in Vygotsky's theory that makes it attractive and relevant more than half a century after its conception?

One reason for the delayed recognition of Vygotsky's theory is that it offered answers to the questions only recently formulated in Western psychology and education.

Alex Kozulin

VIVA VYGOTSKY!

Vygotsky's theory of development is at the same time the theory of education. Jerome Bruner

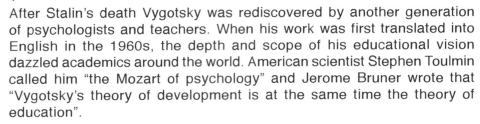

Galina Dolya and Sue Palmer

He lived for only 38 years, but in his last decade (1924–1934), the Russian thinker Lev Vygotsky transformed the study of developmental psychology. His cultural-historical theory caused an explosion of interest in Russia, and inspired much original research by other psychologists.

Tragically, these innovative and inspirational ideas were immediately suppressed. For 20 years after Vygotsky's death it was forbidden to discuss, disseminate or reprint any of his writings. In Stalinist Russia, suggestions for teaching children – indeed anyone – to think for themselves were not acceptable. Vygotsky's works could be read only in a single central library in Moscow by special permission of the secret police.

After Stalin's death Vygotsky was rediscovered by another generation of psychologists and teachers. When his work was first translated into English in the 1960s, the depth and scope of his educational vision dazzled academics around the world. American scientist Stephen Toulmin called him "the Mozart of psychology" and Jerome Bruner wrote that "Vygotsky's theory of development is at the same time the theory of education".

For teachers, Vygotsky provides a theoretical underpinning for effective practice. He identifies the key elements in successful teaching, learning and development – so that one says to oneself, "Ah, that's why I'm doing it! That's what's happening inside the child's head!"

Vygotsky believed that true education is not the mere learning of specific knowledge and skills, it is the development of children's learning abilities – that is, their capacity to think clearly and creatively, plan and implement their plans, and communicate their understanding in a variety of ways. He believed this could be done by providing them with a set of cultural tools for thinking and creating.

The key to human intelligence – the characteristic that makes us different from animals – is the ability to use various types of tools. Vygotsky claimed that, just as humans use material tools (such as knives and levers) to extend our physical abilities, we invented psychological tools to extend our mental abilities. These tools are the symbolic systems we use to communicate and analyse reality. They include signs, symbols, maps, plans, numbers, musical notation, charts, models, pictures and, above all, language.

Cultural tools are not inherited genetically. They are developed and preserved in our culture. Vygotsky believed that the purpose of education is to introduce children to the full range of cultural tools and show how to use them to analyse reality quickly and successfully. Children can then look at the world, as Vygotskian scholar Zaporozhets put it, through "the glasses of human culture". Using cultural tools, children develop new psychological qualities, which we call abilities.

These are the mental habits people need to be successful in particular intellectual or creative fields. The better children's

> *Language gives children a powerful tool that helps them solve difficult tasks, inhibit impulsive actions, plan solutions to problems before executing them, and ultimately, control their own behaviour.*
>
> Lev Vygotsky

grasp of the appropriate cultural tools, the greater their abilities in any field. The development of abilities leads to a flowering of children's personalities. They begin to plan and organise their own activities, openly express their point of view, provide non-standard solutions for problems, interact freely with other people and, most importantly, believe in themselves and their own abilities.

The main premise of Vygotsky's most famous work is the interrelationship between thought and that most universal of cultural tools – language. He maintained that thought is internalised language.

When small children are playing, they often keep up a running commentary on what is happening: "And now the train's going round the tower, and it's banging into the tower, and – oh no – the tower's toppling down ..."

Vygotsky calls this an external monologue. As time goes on, the external monologue is internalised as thought. (When dealing with a challenging situation, children and adults often find it helps to externalise their thoughts again: they begin "thinking aloud" to clarify what they are doing or trying to understand.) The speech structures mastered by children therefore become the basic structures of their thinking.

This means that the development of thought is to a great extent determined by the linguistic ability of the child. This in turn is dependent upon the child's socio-cultural experience – so one of the most important functions of education is to facilitate the development of rich, effective spoken language.

One widely used term from Vygotsky's writing is the zone of proximal development (ZPD). As contemporary Vygotskian scholar Nikolai Veraksa says, the ZPD is "the place where the child and adult meet". Vygotsky believed that the role of the teacher in education is crucial.

In developing children's abilities, teachers can guide them towards performing actions or tasks which are just beyond their current capacity. With such guidance, children can perform beyond their own ability – within certain limits.

Vygotsky defined these limits as the Zone of Proximal Development, which he described as the "difference between the level of solved tasks that can be performed with adult guidance and help, and the level of independently solved tasks". The most effective teaching is aimed at the higher level of the child's ZPD, the edge of challenge.

> Play also creates the Zone of Proximal Development of the child. In play it is though the child were a head taller than his current self and was trying to jump above the head of his normal behaviour. As in the focus of a magnifying glass, play contains all the developed functions in a condensed form.
>
> Lev Vygotsky

The ZPD defines the higher mental functions in a learner that are in the process of maturation, functions that will mature tomorrow but are currently in an embryonic state. They are the "buds"

or "flowers" of development, rather than the "fruits". Vygotsky maintained that conventional measures of educational achievement (for instance, test scores) characterise mental development retrospectively, while the ZPD characterises mental development prospectively. The Vygotskian philosopher Mamardashvili summed it up: "The human being is a possibility."

In his last lecture, *Play and the Psychological Development of the Child*, Vygotsky emphasised the importance of play during the early years: "Play also creates the zone of proximal development of the child. In play, the child is always

behaving beyond his age, above his usual everyday behaviour; in play he is, as it were, a head above himself.

Play contains in a concentrated form, as in the focus of a magnifying glass, all developmental tendencies; it is as if the child tries to jump above his usual level. The relationship of play to development should be compared to the relationship between instruction and development."

In play, children are involved in an imaginary situation, with explicit roles and implicit rules. For instance, when playing "families" they take on clearly understood roles and their actions are determined by those roles. This leads to a greater degree of self-regulation, the children's actions being determined by the rules of the game. When involved in play, children's concentration and application to the task are much greater than in academically-directed activities contrived by the teacher.

After Vygotsky's death, Alexei Leontiev, a fellow Soviet psychologist, crystallised Vygotskian thinking: "Western researchers are constantly seeking to discover how the child came to be what he is. We in Russia are striving to discover not how the child came to be what he is, but how he can become what he not yet is."

> A child's greatest achievements are possible in play, achievements that tomorrow will become his basic level of real action and morality.
>
> What a child can do in cooperation today she can do alone tomorrow. Therefore, the only good kind of instruction is that which marches ahead of development and leads it.
>
> Education must be orientated not towards the yesterday of child development but towards its tomorrow.
>
> Lev Vygotsky

It appears to me that Vygotsky's ideas will facilitate the revival of the public spirit regarding education, making education the talk of the town.

Jacques Carpay

Vygotsky's theory was developed further by outstanding thinkers. However this theory is adequate to its main subject, and the more one develops it, the more work remains. Perhaps, Vygotsky himself should be blamed for having outstripped his time too much.

Vladimir Zinchenko

DEVELOPING LEARNING ABILITIES, UNLOCKING POSSIBILITIES

Being ready for school now doesn't necessarily mean being able to read, write and count, but being ready to learn how to read, write and count.

Leonid Venger

Psychological developments of early childhood are so important that they cannot be left to chance.

Alex Kozulin

- UNDERSTANDING ABILITIES

- THE MECHANISM OF ABILITIES

- THE CLASSIFICATION OF ABILITIES

- A DEVELOPMENTAL CURRICULUM

- TWELVE PROGRAMMES, ONE PRACTICE

- THE PEDAGOGICAL PROCESS

- GROUP WORK

- SUBSTITUTION AND VISUAL MODELLING

- EXTERNAL MEDIATORS: VISIBLE PROPS AND PROMPTS FOR LEARNING

- COGNITIVE TASKS

- VISUAL MODELLING AND PRODUCTIVE IMAGINATION

- IN CONCLUSION

UNDERSTANDING ABILITIES

*We are striving to discover not how the child came to be
'what he is', but how he can become 'what he not yet is'.*
Alexei Leontiev

What are learning abilities? Where do they come from?

The answer to these questions may appear obvious. Learning abilities are whatever it is that determines the speed and flexibility with which we acquire, and are able to apply, new knowledge and skills.

We all know how abilities reveal themselves. Some children are more able than others. They are quick to learn new things, surprise us with their verbal fluency, their precocious achievements in reading and mathematics, in art or in music. If they surprise us enough, we may call them gifted or talented. If they do not, by the time they are seven, we may have decided that they are 'just average' (the majority), or even 'less able' and already marked down for educational failure.

All of us find ourselves thinking about and judging young children's different abilities in this way from time to time. We also tend to believe that while children's educational and life experiences may affect for better or for worse the way they put their abilities to use, the abilities themselves are a given. We behave as though they are a part of our genetic inheritance, like the colour of our eyes, or the number of fingers on our hands.

However, Vygotsky considered that we must view human psychological development as a social achievement rather than an individual one. Young children's abilities are not innate, or simply determined by biology. Children acquire their abilities with and from the others around them – from the social, cultural and educational context of their lives.

DEVELOPMENT OF HIGHER MENTAL FUNCTIONS

LOWER FUNCTIONS Inborn, shared with higher animals	**HIGHER FUNCTIONS** Unique to humans, passed on by teaching
REACTIVE ATTENTION	FOCUSSED ATTENTION
ASSOCIATIVE MEMORY	DELIBERATE MEMORY
SENSORIMOTOR THOUGHT	SYMBOLIC THOUGHT

The core of what young children learn is not a particular body of knowledge or a specific set of skills. After all, the skills and knowledge children need for survival depend on where they happen to be born, and vary from place to place.

At the heart of what all young children learn, are the universal higher mental functions required to analyse reality. How deeply and securely children are able to acquire them ultimately determines differences in their abilities.

Leonid Venger, Olga Diachenko, Nickolai Veraksa and other Russian psychologists and educationalists extended and adapted Vygotsky's ideas about learning and development in young children. Their work has led to the development of principles, curriculum content and methods aimed at developing the cognitive abilities of young children (age three to seven). The approach makes it possible to substantially increase the developmental effect of education and its influence on the development of cognitive abilities.

> From a Vygotskian point of view the essence of cognitive education lies in providing students with new psychological tools that can shape either general or more domain-specific cognitive functions.
>
> Alex Kozulin

THE MECHANISM OF ABILITIES

The child looks at the world through the glasses of Human Culture. Alexander Zaporozhets

Children learn to "read" reality through the glasses of human culture. These glasses are cultural tools, for example, concepts, visual signs, symbols, models, plans, texts, maps, formulae, and above all language. It is these that provide us with the universal "mental habits" and human qualities required for success in

SYMBOLIC TOOLS

MAPS		CHARTS	
PLANS		GRAPHS	
SCHEMAS		FORMULAE	$F=ma$
DIAGRAMS		SIGNS	
TABLES		SYMBOLS	
NUMBERS	1 2 3 4 5	LETTERS	ABC
MUSICAL NOTATION		MODELS	

any skilled cultural activity. It is through these tools that new psychological qualities that we call abilities emerge.

This is not a passive process but an active appropriation. Where the process is at its best, cultural symbolic tools are not merely learned in isolation as skills, but offered to and grasped by children as purposeful practical activity. When children are able to take over symbolic tools so that they own them, they develop the ability not simply to solve conventional problems in old ways, but to innovate and sometimes to change or create the tools themselves.

Creativity and independent thought are not where we start. They are the results of our learning.

> According to Vygotsky, the acquisition of cultural tools, such as language, signs and concepts constitutes the main content of the child's mental development.
>
> Arievitch and Stetsenko

THE CLASSIFICATION OF ABILITIES

Abilities are those qualities that provide successful learning.
Nikolai Veraksa

When we think about what our children might be good at, we often have in mind a specific list. For example, we might think about Linguistic, Mathematical, Musical, Physical, Visual, Intra-personal or Inter-personal abilities. The Russian psychologists Olga Diachenko and Nickolai Veraksa stress that young children must develop communicative, self-regulative and cognitive abilities. Children need to be able to understand others and to make themselves understood. They need to be able to plan and to manage their own attention and behaviour. And they need to be able to build mental models of how the world works. These are the general abilities we need. They are the learning abilities that are the prerequisites for success at school and for creative and intellectual achievement.

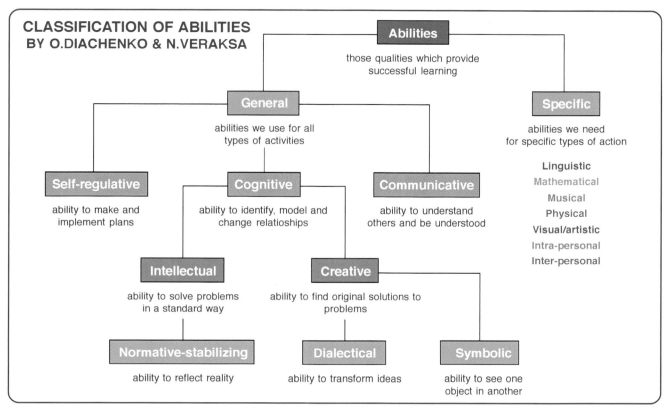

CLASSIFICATION OF ABILITIES
BY O.DIACHENKO & N.VERAKSA

Abilities
those qualities which provide successful learning

General
abilities we use for all types of activities

Specific
abilities we need for specific types of action

Linguistic
Mathematical
Musical
Physical
Visual/artistic
Intra-personal
Inter-personal

Self-regulative
ability to make and implement plans

Cognitive
ability to identify, model and change relatioships

Communicative
ability to understand others and be understood

Intellectual
ability to solve problems in a standard way

Creative
ability to find original solutions to problems

Normative-stabilizing
ability to reflect reality

Dialectical
ability to transform ideas

Symbolic
ability to see one object in another

The Key to Learning curriculum offers a unique and specific approach to the development of cognitive abilities. It focuses equally on the development of each of this trio of general learning abilities – communication, self-regulation and cognition – because all three are equally important.

A DEVELOPMENTAL CURRICULUM

Education must be oriented not towards the yesterday of a child's development, but towards its tomorrow. Lev Vygotsky

According to the Russian psychologist Alexander Zaporozhets, there are two parallel cultural universes – the adult's and the child's. Consequently, there are two possible approaches for child educators. We can attempt to take children by the scruff of the neck and drag them into the adult culture, attempting to move them prematurely to the next stage of development. Alternatively, we can allow children to live through their childhood as fully as possible, but work to help them deepen and enrich their child's eye view. Here we have the essence of a concept known as "developmental education."

> A child's greatest achievements are possible in play, achievements that tomorrow will become his basic level of real action and morality...
>
> It is the essence of play that a new relation is created... between situations in thought and real situations.
>
> Lev Vygotsky

A developmental curriculum must help children to move forward. To do this it must provide challenging experiences that are enjoyable and achievable given the right support. This is what we mean by teaching within the child's learning zone (the "Zone of Proximal Development"). For young children it is imaginative play that creates the learning zone. As Vygotsky points out, children's greatest achievements are possible in play. It is in play that children become "a head taller" than their current selves; they leap ahead of their everyday capability. For example, impulsive children who cannot sit still during circle time may be able to stand still for quite a long time if they are pretending to be guards at the palace gates.

> Research from a veriety of theoretical perspectives suggests that a defining feature of a supportive environment is a responsible and responsive adult.
>
> Parents, teachers and carers promote development when they create learning experiences that build on and extend the child's competence – experiences that are challenging but within reach.
>
> When educational activities operate in the child's "Zone of Proximal Development" where learning is within the reach but takes the child just beyond her existing ability these curricula have been reported as being both enjoyable and educational.
>
> Eager to Learn:
> Educating our Preschoolers
> Report of National Research Council
> of the USA, November 2000

The Key to Learning Curriculum builds on features of young children's spontaneous activity to promote active learning. Prominent Russian psychologists and educationalists, led by Leonid Venger, Olga Diachenko and Nickolai Veraksa have developed principles, curriculum content and methods that amplify the world children naturally inhabit to make sure that they explore every corner of it in as

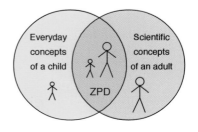

much depth as possible. Although the aim of the Key to Learning curriculum is to help children develop communicative, self-regulative and cognitive abilities, it does this indirectly, through sequences of planned activities that are emotionally vibrant, playful and enjoyable. Only the teacher knows that teaching is going on.

TWELVE PROGRAMMES, ONE PRACTICE

Key to Learning

According to Vygotsky, psychological development occurs through teaching/learning and upbringing using various types of spontaneous and specially organised interactions of the child with adults – interactions through which a human being assimilates the achievements of historically shaped culture. An essential role in this process is played by systems of signs and symbols. Vasily Davydov

In terms of content the Developmental Cognitive Curriculum Key to Learning offers breadth and diversity for children between the ages of 3 and 7. There are twelve programmes in the complete curriculum.

SENSORY MATHEMATICS

develops the ability to analyse the external, visual qualities of objects using sensory standards such as colour, shape and size. It builds the foundation for the development of mental abilities

LOGIC

develops the ability to analyse objects and events, see their invisible sides, identify their most essential characteristics, think sequentially, draw conclusions, classify and systematise information

MATHEMATICS

using visual models children discover the language of Mathematics and the concept of measurement, compare different quantities and qualities of objects and explore the relationships *more, less* and *equal*

STORY GRAMMAR

develops a love of story, ownership of story language and a profound understanding of story structure by following a specific set of procedures known as visual modelling

DEVELOPMENTAL GAMES

playing in small and large groups children develop productive imagination, symbolic literacy, language and communication skills, flexible thinking, creative problem solving, self-regulation and self-esteem

ARTOGRAPHICS

cultivates the essential skills required both for writing and creative artistic expression, Develops "art vision" and introduces different symbolic tools – composition, rhythm and colour

VISUAL-SPATIAL

develops spatial awareness and the ability to "read" maps. Children look at objects in space and use symbols to represent what they and others see through visual models – maps, schemes and plans

CREATIVE MODELLING

through shared activity children discover symmetry and pattern by manipulating geometric shapes to create artistic compositions representing the world around them. Develops co-operative and social skills

CONSTRUCTION

develops mathematical language and goal directed behaviour. Children analyse the structure of objects, plan, articulate their plans and execute them using wooden modular building blocks

EXPLORATION

through games, stories and simple yet powerful experiments children discover important scientific concepts – states of matter, different qualities of substances and transformations

EXPRESSIVE MOVEMENT

develops emotional intelligence, non-verbal communication skills, creativity and productive imagination through body movement, gestures, facial expressions and music

YOU – ME – WORLD

using symbols and visual models children learn about themselves as physical, emotional and social beings; about the natural and material world, about living things and inanimate objects

Each programme consists of 60 sessions: 30 for younger children (Caterpillars), 30 for older children (Butterflies). It provides opportunities for child-initiated and teacher-structured activities. There are, in addition, suggestions for follow up activities that can be shared with parents.

	CATERPILLARS	BUTTERFLIES
1	Story Grammar	Story Grammar
2	Story Grammar	Visual-Spatial
3	Expressive Movement	Expressive Movement
4	Developmental Games	Developmental Games
5	Creative Modelling	Creative Modelling
6	Artographics	Artographics
7	Sensory Maths	Mathematics
8	Sensory Maths	Logic
9	Construction	Construction
10	You – Me – World	Exploration

Day Planner — MONDAY

	Butterflies	Butterflies	Caterpillars	Caterpillars
$09^{15} - 09^{30}$	Rainbow and Brain Gym			
$09^{35} - 09^{45}$	Learning Circle			
$09^{50} - 10^{10}$	Visual-spatial	Artographics	Self-Directed Play	
$10^{15} - 10^{30}$	Artographics	Visual-spatial		
$10^{35} - 11^{20}$	Snack and Outdoor Play			
$11^{25} - 11^{40}$	Self-Directed Play		Construction	Sensory Maths
$11^{45} - 12^{00}$			Sensory Maths	Construction
$12^{05} - 12^{15}$	Story Time			

The programmes form a coherent whole: they have a particular view of the role of the teacher; they emphasise group work; and they offer young children opportunities to master five types of cognitive task. Each programme contributes in differing proportions to the six areas of the Early Years Foundation Stage: Communication, Language and Literacy; Problem Solving, Reasoning and Numeracy; Creative Development; Knowledge and Understanding of the World; Personal, Social and Emotional Development and Physical Development. The Curriculum is already being implemented in a large number of schools in England, Scotland, Russia, Poland and Singapore. Independent research has shown that the effect on the performance of the children is remarkable.

EARLY LEARNING GOALS	DEVELOPMENTAL COGNITIVE CURRICULUM				
Personal, Social and Emotional Development	DEVELOPMENTAL GAMES	YOU-ME-WORLD	CREATIVE MODELLING	EXPRESSIVE MOVEMENT	STORY GRAMMAR
Communication, Language and Literacy	STORY GRAMMAR	ARTOGRAPHICS	DEVELOPMENTAL GAMES	YOU-ME-WORLD	CREATIVE MODELLING
Problem Solving, Reasoning and Numeracy	SENSORY MATHEMATICS	MATHEMATICS AND LOGIC	CONSTRUCTION	CREATIVE MODELLING	VISUAL SPATIAL
Knowledge and Understanding of the World	EXPLORATION	YOU-ME-WORLD	VISUAL SPATIAL	CONSTRUCTION	CREATIVE MODELLING
Physical Development	EXPRESSIVE MOVEMENT	ARTOGRAPHICS	DEVELOPMENTAL GAMES	CREATIVE MODELLING	CONSTRUCTION
Creative Development	DEVELOPMENTAL GAMES	CREATIVE MODELLING	ARTOGRAPHICS	EXPRESSIVE MOVEMENT	CONSTRUCTION

THE PEDAGOGICAL PROCESS

Children do not just happen to re-invent the knowledge of centuries. Edwards and Mercer

Culture is not discovered; it is passed on or forgotten.
Jerome Bruner

> What a child can do in cooperation today she can do alone tomorrow. Therefore, the only good kind of instruction is that which marches ahead of development and leads it .
>
> Lev Vygotsty

PEDAGOGICAL PROCESS

TEACHING MODEL	COOPERATION MODEL	AUTONOMOUS MODEL
RELATIONSHIP ADULT – CHILD		
Expert and apprentice	Collaborators	Independent learners and observer

FORM AND STRUCTURE OF THE EDUCATIONAL PROCESS		
Teacher invites, initiates games, models and mediates mental tools, facilitates, discusses, and promotes reflection	Teacher and children play together and create through joint activity	Teacher organises the environment, observes spontaneous self initiated play and supports if necessary

The Key to Learning approach recognises three types of learning and teaching process. During sessions teachers lead short bursts of structured activity. Sometimes they share their expertise with children, modelling and mediating the use of mental tools through developmentally appropriate and engaging activity. At other times, perhaps during the same session, the teacher and children collaborate to create something together, through joint activity. Finally, the expectation is that the children will continue to

> Properly organized instruction will result in the child's intellectual development, will bring into being an entire series of such developmental proces-ses, which were not at all possible without instruction.
>
> Lev Vygotsty

do what they already do, spending much of their time engaged in spontaneous free choice play, under the watchful eye of a facilitating adult. Of course, at such times, teachers are free to enrich the range of available choices by leaving relevant materials from recent sessions available for the children to use independently.

GROUP WORK

It is only through others that we become ourselves.
Lev Vygotsky

Group work is an important component of the Key to Learning approach. The most obvious, common sense reason for this is that the ability to work co-operatively as part of a group is essential if a child is to make a smooth transition to formal schooling; if we wish to foster communication and co-operation we must provide rich opportunities for practice.

Less obviously, but perhaps more profoundly, working in a group offers children the opportunity to reflect on other children's opinions. Toddlers are very egocentric, subjective and one sided in their understanding of things and their perception of the world around them.

They sincerely believe that anything they see really is exactly as they see it at that moment, from where they are standing. It is not possible for them to understand that from the other side, from a different place, a thing may look different; that something is the same thing from both sides rather than two different things. Even if they walk around it many times they are not sensitive to contradictions.

If one child gives one answer and another a different answer, it begins to open up the possibility of putting oneself in another's place and seeing things from another's perspective.

SUBSTITUTION AND VISUAL MODELLING

The ability to distil our everyday experience in useful maps and models of the world around us is very down-to-earth: so mundane is it that it is, in many ways, the unsung hero of the cognitive repertoire. *Guy Claxton*

The models or schemas of the 'hidden' rational structure of the objects and their essential relationships, once they are internalised by children, become a key part of children's orientation in a broad subject domain. As new powerful cognitive tools, these models qualitatively change the child's whole way of viewing things, thinking about things, and operating with things in a given domain. In fact, they advance the child's cognitive development to a new, unusually high level. *Arievitch and Stetsenko*

Visual models of different connections and relations are optimal means of presenting preschoolers with generalised knowledge of space, natural phenomena and the development of primary mathematics and linguistic concepts. *Leonid Venger*

Vygotsky emphasised the need to teach the function of symbolisation prior to engaging children into the specific techniques of writing and spelling.
Alex Kozulin

People have invented countless signs and symbols, and there are rules to be learned that allow us to use them correctly. But the first and the most important difficulty we have to overcome lies not in learning the rules themselves but in understanding what they mean, and which side of reality is hidden behind them. Visual Modelling makes learning and thinking visible so that children can see the underlying hidden reality.

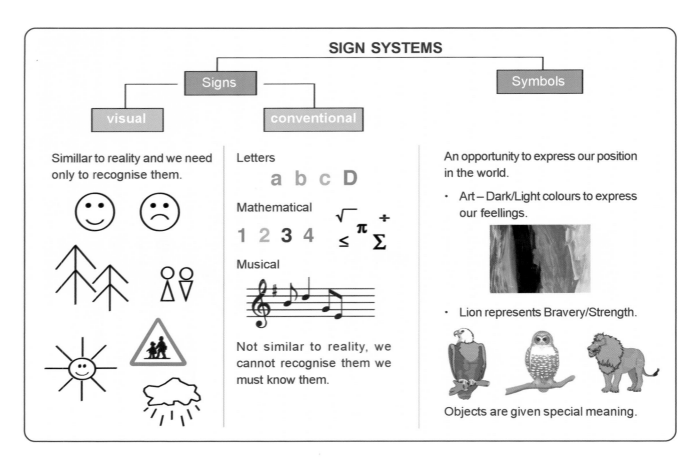

Substitution is the use of conventional substitutes (signs and symbols) instead of real objects or phenomena to solve problems. It first appears spontaneously in children's play. For instance, a building block becomes the soap a child uses to wash; a child transforms a chair into a car by sitting on it and making sounds to represent a motor working. Objects are used to substitute for other objects – a stick may become a thermometer, spoon, gun or even a horse.

> A symbol is the bird's eye view of the area.
>
> Thinkers are those who see everything from the bird's eye view.
>
> Nikolai Veraksa

The substitution and visual modelling that take place in play are embryonic forms of the cognitive abilities that lead ultimately to the development and understanding of mathematical symbols, musical notation, and computer programmes.

However, the most important impact these activities have at first is in enabling young children to understand the true meaning of the words that identify characteristic features of objects and phenomena. They help young children come to grips with the everyday realities of the world about them.

Later they have a crucial role in successful problem solving. To solve any problem we must identify, analyse and take into account all the relevant conditions and the relationships. For

> Modelling is recognised as the central action of the learning activity because it helps students hold together and consider simultaneously the object and ideas about the nature and origin of these objects.
>
> Vasily Davydov

example, in mathematical problems we consider the relationship between quantities; in problems of spatial orientation – the relationship between positions occupied by various objects in space (behind, in front, to the left, etc.), and in relation to the spatial axes. We can express such relationships either verbally or by using a model where the objects themselves are represented by conventional substitutes and their relationships by the positioning of the substitutes in space.

CATERPILLARS   **EXPLORATION**

WHO LIVES HERE?

AIMS

- To develop the ability to use symbols to represent an adult and a child.
- To develop the ability to construct representations of a house and family.
- To use representations of a house and a family.
- To develop the concept of an address.
- To learn their address – the number of the house and the name of the road.
- To develop the ability to use substitute shapes to represent real objects.

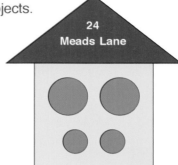

LEARNING OUTCOMES

Children can use symbols to represent adult and child.

Children can recognise a representation of a house and family.

Children know their address – the number of the house and the name of the road.

CATERPILLARS   **YOU – ME – WORLD**

MORNING – AFTERNOON (DAY) – EVENING – NIGHT

AIMS

- To understand the concept of time.
- To built and use the model of the whole day.
- To understand the concept 'between'.
- To develop the concept 'circle'.
- To develop the ability to classify.

LEARNING OUTCOMES

Each child can explain what hapens at different times of the day.

Children can understand the concept of substitution of symbols for real objects.

A concentrated focus on helping young children to understand symbols and to use them to create models is doubly appropriate. In the first place we are taking advantage of what is, in any case, natural spontaneous activity. Secondly we are tapping into the young child's relative strength as a visual thinker. Young children can understand and solve problems if they can "see" them.

Nevertheless, substitution is not just confined to objects. Children transform themselves in role-play, acting out the part of another person (a doctor, a mother, a character from the TV). Role-play is particularly significant in this context, because in role-play children practise both substitution and modelling. They are enabled to think about relationships between adults as they actively model those relationships in their games.

Visual Modelling is a common feature of young children's drawings. Their drawings are schematic. They do not depict the general appearance of an object as such. Rather they convey what the child understands about the structure of the object, the relationship between an object's main parts and the relationships between objects.

In other words the children create images which are closer to visual models than photographs. For example, when children impersonate a patient and a doctor they in fact create a model of the doctor-patient relationship, even though this model is not represented on paper but unfolds in action.

Similarly children produce three-dimensional models of real buildings during construction activities. A house made out of building blocks is in itself a visual model. It expresses by means of substitutes (building blocks) the relationships between the main components (walls, the roof, windows, doors).

> During two to five epoch making events occur in the child's symbolic development. The child is involved in the mastering and the development of diverse symbol systems.
>
> The child of five indeed has attained a first draft knowledge of numerous symbolic products. Indeed, this age is often described as a flowering of symbolic activity, for the child can enthusiastically and effortlessly produce instances in each of these symbolic domains.
>
> Howard Gardner

As preschool children typically use substitutes for various objects and construct visual models spontaneously it is undoubtedly true that any normal child will master these processes to some degree without any special educational influence. However, without planned and appropriate influence from adults, there is likely to be considerable

variation in how quickly children develop abilities, how well they develop them, and how often they practise using them. We cannot afford to leave to chance how well the vital trio of general learning abilities develops – communication, self-regulation and cognition. Some children will not develop their full potential; others may be left behind completely.

The Key to Learning Curriculum provides special tasks that encourage young children to use different types of substitutes for various objects and to develop a wide range of visual models. These developmentally appropriate tasks, presented in a developmentally appropriate manner, can considerably increase the level of communicative, self-regulative and cognitive abilities for all children.

EXTERNAL MEDIATORS
VISIBLE PROPS AND PROMPTS FOR LEARNING

Visual Modelling makes learning and thinking visible so that children can see the process. Olga Diachenko

The maps in the Visual-Spatial programme, the substitute shapes in Sensory Mathematics, the Venn Diagrams in Logic, the Story Skeletons in Story Grammar, the 2D diagrams in Construction are, in effect, external mediators which help children to internalise challenging concepts.

The Key to Learning Curriculum also employs a range of additional external mediators across all the programmes, specifically aimed at supporting the development of self-regulation, deliberate memory and focussed attention.

Young children frequently depend on regulation by others (parents and teachers); but what happens if the adult moves away and the child cannot remember what to do, or maintain motivation and focus?

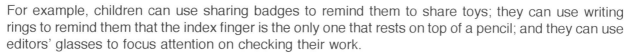

We can help the child to succeed by providing external mediators – tangible, visible reminders – to scaffold particular behaviours (don't bite), focussed attention (check what you have done) and deliberate memory (do this first, then that).

For example, children can use sharing badges to remind them to share toys; they can use writing rings to remind them that the index finger is the only one that rests on top of a pencil; and they can use editors' glasses to focus attention on checking their work.

Some external mediators are in fact not visible objects. They may be words ("indoor voices please" as a reminder to speak quietly inside the classroom), rituals (a set of well known procedures for clearing up after play), sounds (e.g. songs that open and close circle time, bells to signal the end of the morning) or gestures (e.g. a raised hand to gather attention).

Such mediators are prompts that help the child to become more independent; they bridge the gap between acting only when prompted by an adult and acting out of an internalised intention. Unlike the maps, plans, diagrams, schemes and other cultural tools, these mediators will eventually be outgrown and (usually) discarded.

COGNITIVE TASKS

Learning activity presupposes the development of theoretical thinking, the basis of which is a system of scientific concepts. For five-year-old children, however, logical-conceptual forms of cognition are not nearly as typical as visual-representational ones. Venger & Gorbov

The Key to Learning Curriculum is based on helping children to achieve mastery of five types of cognitive tasks:

- The substitution of objects
- The analysis of the structure of objects
- Identification of spatial relationships
- The utilisation of logical relationships
- The creation of new images

The substitution of objects

The first type of task offered to children is aimed at developing the ability to use a variety of substitutes to represent a variety of objects. In some tasks features of the substitute bear some resemblance to features of the real objects to which they refer. In other tasks the substitutes are purely conventional. These tasks develop children's ability to perform the action of substitution and to match objects to appropriate substitutes. This type of problem includes solving verbal riddles where children must recognise objects on the basis of verbal descriptions of their characteristic features.

 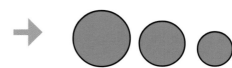

The analysis of the structure of objects and the identification of spatial relationships

Both these types of tasks are aimed at developing the concept of visual modelling. Children learn to use visual models (diagrams, drawings, plans) to represent spatial relationships between different objects or between the different parts of a single object.). The focus is on helping children to make the connection between the visual models and the reality they represent; making sure they can spell out exactly the form the connection takes (e.g. circles represent wheels because both are round); and making sure they can make use of the same connection in independent activities.

The utilisation of logical relationships

The fourth type of task develops the ability to perform logical operations, i.e. to group objects or their spatial arrangements on the basis of given characteristics. These tasks are based on analysing and identifying the most important features of objects or their spatial arrangements. In this case the visual models themselves allow children to "see" the act of classification they represent.

The creation of new images

The fifth type of task is aimed at developing productive imagination. These tasks are based on using substitutes (signs and symbols) and visual models to create new images. In these tasks children are engaged in a process of solving imaginative problems, for example creating their own drawings, representations, stories, fairytales, etc. either independently or in collaboration with others. Since all tasks aimed at developing productive imagination allow variable solutions it is vitally important to be positive about any solutions or suggestions children make during games and activities, particularly in the initial stages. If teachers want to maintain active participation and avoid discouraging originality they must be careful to increase their expectations of the quality of children's suggestions very gradually.

To gain maximum benefit from the curriculum they must also ensure that they maintain a regular weekly schedule of structured educational activity.

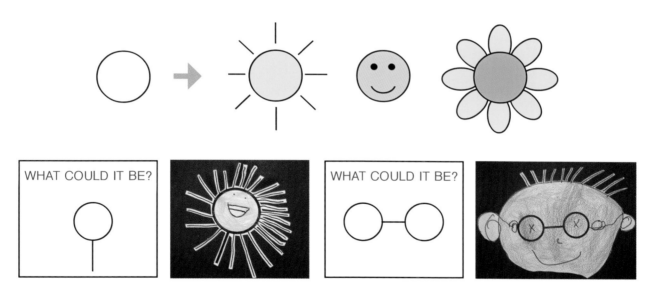

VISUAL MODELLING AND PRODUCTIVE IMAGINATION

The child's cognitive abilities are determined by the level of development of two inverse processes: visual modelling and productive imagination. Nikolai Veraksa

According to Venger, the ability to generate these models, understand them and use them makes it possible for young children to develop general cognitive competencies and constitutes one of the major developmental accomplishments of the preschool age. Bodrova and Leong

A child confident with external forms of substitution and visual modelling (who can use symbols, drawings, diagrams, plans) becomes capable of using substitutes and visual models mentally. With their help he/she is able to process the information offered by adults, visualising the results of his/her actions in advance. These are the qualities characteristic of a high level of development of cognitive abilities. Olga Diachenko

Visual Modelling – the ability to "translate" information into a visual model using substitutes (signs and symbols) – facilitates intellectual problem solving. We learn to solve many problems using mental strategies to consider our options and make plans, rather than relying on trial and error procedures with real objects.

The other side of this coin is the development of creativity. Once we are able to decode the meanings of signs and symbols, and to comprehend the models others have created, we are free to reinterpret and to reinvent, to see in diverse ways. In coming to own the process of modelling, we gain the freedom to create our own models.

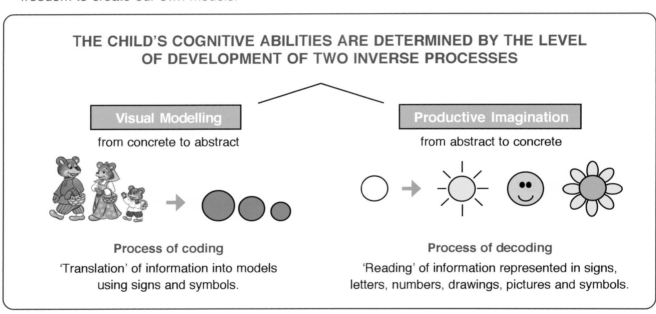

THE CHILD'S COGNITIVE ABILITIES ARE DETERMINED BY THE LEVEL OF DEVELOPMENT OF TWO INVERSE PROCESSES

Visual Modelling
from concrete to abstract

Productive Imagination
from abstract to concrete

Process of coding
'Translation' of information into models using signs and symbols.

Process of decoding
'Reading' of information represented in signs, letters, numbers, drawings, pictures and symbols.

IN CONCLUSION

...at this age it is not yet a learning activity as such that should be developed, but rather its prerequisites. Venger & Gorbov

The Key to Learning Curriculum is unique because it moves focus from educational content (what) to the cultural tools and pedagogical practice (how). It focuses not only on teaching children skills and knowledge but on developing learning abilities. It offers optimal learning experiences that are:

- precisely matched to children's learning and development
- challenging but attainable
- emotionally vibrant, playful and enjoyable
- shared by children and responsive adults

It creates the right conditions for minds to open, for learning to become a pleasure and for creativity to flourish.

FROM SENSORY STANDARDS TO VERBAL REASONING

A THEORETICAL PERSPECTIVE

Children learn algebra first in order to organise their thinking processes. Mathematics (number) comes after.

Alex Kozulin

- **SENSORY STANDARDS AND PERCEPTUAL MODELLING**

- **CREATIVE MODELLING**

- **MATHEMATICS**

- **LOGIC**

- **CONSTRUCTION**

The beauty and coherence of the Key to Learning Developmental Cognitive Curriculum stems from the years of observation and reflection that have gone into the development of its theoretical underpinnings. We have included this chapter to allow those practitioners who are interested to take a closer look at some aspects of the curriculum from a theoretical perspective. We believe that many teachers will find that engagement with the theory is both challenging and empowering, enabling them to reflect on their work and to become freer and more creative in their interpretation and modification of the curriculum.

However, please bear in mind that a love of theory is not essential! If you are short of time or prefer getting down to the nitty-gritty of practical application, simply skip this chapter. You will find that the sessions themselves are exciting, enjoyable, easy to follow and, above all, very effective.

SENSORY STANDARDS AND PERCEPTUAL MODELLING

The pre-school period is characterised by transition from the acquisition of isolated standards to practical mastery, internalisation and automatic application of the system of sensory standards. This process plays a decisive role in the child's mental development. Leonid Venger

The Key to Learning technology of the development of cognitive abilities is based on a systematic introduction to sensory standards and perceptual modelling.

Perception is the first step in learning about the world. It is the foundation for memory, thinking and imagination. When young children engage in playful activity – building, drawing or pretend play – they begin with perception. They focus on the external properties of objects. For example, a child playing with a doll may use a stick as the "spoon" with which to feed it and the stick will be chosen because of the properties it shares with a real spoon (long and thin).

From the age of about three, this focus on the external properties of objects begins to develop intensively as young children embark on the long process of transforming perception through the active acquisition of sensory standards.

The natural world is almost overwhelmingly rich in its diversity of colours, shapes and forms. Our senses give us the ability to perceive this diversity, but it is culture that teaches us to make sense of

our perceptions. We do not see, hear and feel directly but with the help of special "glasses" – internalised sensory standards for colour, size and shape.

For example, if we take a familiar object such as a lemon and describe its visual properties we might say, "Lemons are yellow and oval". Because this description is so obvious and familiar, we rarely stop to consider that to make it we employ two sensory standards – colour and shape. We forget that to make the statement we must call on our prior experience with objects that are yellow (e.g. daffodils) and with objects that are oval (e.g. eggs). The lemon does not

summon these descriptive labels all by itself – it is not the carrier of sensory standards. Our culture – the accumulated experience of the social world into which we are born with its language and concepts – is the carrier of those standards.

Sensory abilities, shaped by our cultures, are the foundation upon which mental development builds.

We lay this foundation by internalising sensory standards for colour, shape and size against which we can compare all the objects we encounter. These standards do much more than provide a point of comparison. When we internalise sensory standards we come to recognise that the perceptual properties of objects – and particularly their visual properties – have characteristics that can be organised and classified. This systematisation allows us to make sense of the world and to operate confidently within it.

Consequently, it is crucial for educators to pay close attention to the opportunities we offer young children to grasp, comprehend and own the sensory standards. It is through interaction with others that we learn how to look, what to look at, and to consider our reasons for looking. Moreover, if educators plan those interactions carefully they can help to ensure strong foundations for cognitive development.

It is clear that a child cannot acquire these systems all at once. Children acquire sensory standards in the same way as they acquire the language system. And, as with language acquisition, the process is gradual and personal, marked with errors and contradictions which, over time, children come to notice and to eliminate as their understanding and proficiency develop.

Stages of acquisition of sensory standards

The acquisition of sensory standards helps the child to analyse objects and their relationships via culturally defined standards of colour, shape and size. It happens over a long period and goes through several stages.

Pre-standard stage

Children begin to acquire sensory standards and to use them in early childhood. They learn about the standards as they manipulate and play with objects, because standards are widely represented in the features and characteristics of the everyday objects with which they come into contact. They have to take the perceptual features of objects into account to be able to act on them effectively!

Children usually begin to focus on visual perceptual characteristics in the third year of life when the leading activity is the manipulation of objects. During this stage, children tend to use a single object as the standard for some salient perceptual feature. Thus, all green objects may be "grass", all yellow objects "the sun". Similarly, a child may call all triangular objects "roof" and say that all round objects look like "a ball". During this stage, as a result of their manipulation of objects, children will begin to internalise the characteristic qualities implicit in the external properties of the objects, e.g. you cannot put a ball on a "roof" – it will fall off.

Transitional stage to sensory standards

Between 3 and 4 most children begin the transition from the use of single objects as standards of comparison to sensory standards. When they describe an object, they no longer rely on their perception of some specific concrete object but begin to internalise perceptual qualities that have their own defined names. They are ready to begin the Sensory Mathematics programme.

Throughout this programme, sensory standards are represented in social experiences not as isolated patterns of sensory qualities. The goal is for children eventually to grasp the standards as systems – patterns constructed in a certain order.

Children following the Sensory Mathematics programme will acquire the main colours of the spectrum both through everyday activity (free-flow play) and during specially organised activities, e.g. the children hide mice from the cat by selecting from a collection of different coloured doors the one that exactly matches the colour of the house in which their mouse has taken shelter. In this case, the colour of the house is the sensory standard for the colour of the door. (Choose the red door for the house that is the same red colour).

The main sensory standards of shape are geometrical – square, circle, triangle, oval and rectangle. The programme introduces these through games. For example, the Shape People live in the Kingdom of Shapes. Their names are Square, Circle, Triangle, Rectangle, and Oval.

Children use these shape people as perceptual standards for the shapes of a variety of different objects (biscuits, handkerchiefs, plates) which children present to the Shape People (each one has a preference for objects in its own image: Circle likes everything round, Square – everything square, etc.). It is important to recognise that these games and activities are not intended to teach the children to name shapes and colours in the first instance. The teacher uses the correct names but the focus for the child is to pay attention to the visual properties of the objects whilst performing actions with them.

Naming the property comes later as an end product of the internalisation of the perceptual feature and has the function of generalisation and consolidation. Later, if a child says, "I want a round red balloon," we can be confident that the child understands exactly the perceptual reality behind those words.

The sensory standard of size is of course a special case because it is conventional. Objects cannot be big or small on their own; they acquire this quality in comparison to other objects. Although there is an internationally accepted standard of size (the metric system), we do not use it at the perceptual level. Instead, we use looser vocabulary. We say that an elephant is big and a fly is small when we compare them with each other. In this case, ideas about the relative sizes of objects are indicated by words which point to their place in a row (or series) of others (the biggest, big, middle sized, small, the smallest). In this case, children point to concrete objects in order to assess their relative size, but internalisation of the standard depends on acquiring the verbal forms and being able to use them correctly.

Systematisation of sensory standards

By this time, the children begin to systematise sensory standards. In terms of colour, the task of the teacher is to help the children understand the sequence of the colours of the spectrum and to recognise their shades; to help them learn about how we change a colour into a variation of a different shade; to help them group colours as warm or cold, soft or bright; and to introduce their emotional connotations.

In terms of shape, the programme introduces variations of geometric shapes – right angled, acute angled, obtuse angled triangles; rectangles which have different proportions of length and width. At this stage, the focus is still perceptual, i.e. the children are not yet ready for mathematical analysis.

From a general evaluation of the size of objects (big – small) children move to the identification of different parameters of size: height, width and length; and they practise building seriation rows. Accordingly, the games become more complex, e.g. children are given two ribbons of different length and are asked to tie bows on two identical Teddy Bears.

Of course it will be easier to tie the bow with the longer ribbon because the shorter one will not go round the Teddy Bear's neck far enough to make a bow. Therefore, the children analyse the constraint that prevents the goal being achieved: the ribbon is too short, they need a longer one (they come to this conclusion by the direct comparison of one ribbon with the other). Thus, the game enables children to single out the requisite parameter (length) on the perceptual level.

To introduce children to sensory standards ultimately means to teach them to remember those words that identify or express the main perceptual qualities of objects. Mastery of vocabulary helps children remember the sensory standards and enables them to use the standards more precisely. However, just showing children objects in a variety of different geometrical shapes, colours and sizes and asking them to remember the names will not help the children to master the system of sensory standards – even if they do manage to learn the labels.

We need to introduce the names of the sensory standards in context, as part of a sequence of practical and engaging activities, where the requirements of the activities themselves direct children's attention to the relevant standards and keep it focussed there.

In relation to acquiring sensory standards there are three kinds of actions which children need to master at a perceptual level.

The action of identification

Children compare several objects, using given criteria to find those which are identical to each other e.g. in the game "Hide the Mouse" the children learn to identify the correct door (identical colour) for the house by the process of imposing the door on the house and checking to see if they are identical.

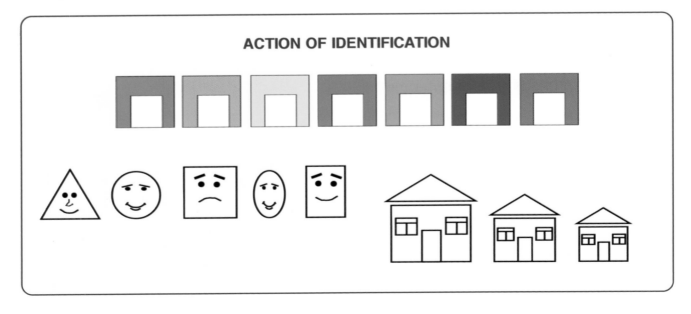

ACTION OF IDENTIFICATION

CATERPILLARS   **SENSORY MATHS - 1**

HIDE THE MOUSE

AIMS

- To develop colour recognition with reference to the seven colours of the spectrum: red, orange, yellow, green, blue, indigo, and violet.
- To practise matching colours to a sensory standard.

LEARNING OUTCOMES

Children match doors to houses of the same colour.

Children distinguish between the 7 colours of the spectrum when choosing the doors.

The action of comparison

Children compare several objects and group those which are similar, but not necessarily identical, e.g. in the game *Shape Money* the "shopkeeper" needs to "sell" the "customer" an object (a toy) which is the same shape as the coin presented to him. The object looks similar to the coin (they are the same shape) but is not identical.

To find the right object the "shopkeeper" needs to compare the object with the sensory standard – the coin. If superimposition is impossible (the object is 3D or differs significantly from the standard), children can trace the contour of the object or standard with a finger and watch the movement of their hand try to find the similarity between the object and the standard.

ACTION OF COMPARISON

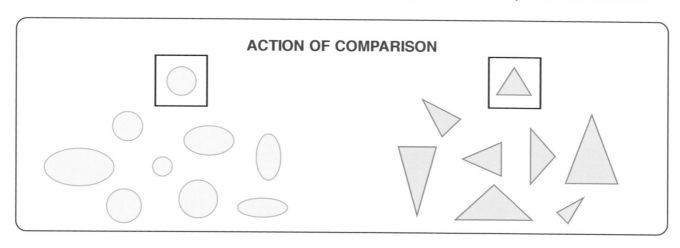

CATERPILLARS   **SENSORY MATHS - 22**

SHAPE FAMILIES – TRIANGLES, SQUARES AND RECTANGLES

AIMS

- To develop shape recognition (distinguish between squares, triangles and rectangles).
- To develop categorisation (droup by geometric shape, regardless of colour and size).
- To review a kinaesthetic procedure for exploring shapes.
- To develop the ability to compare shapes to a sensory standard.

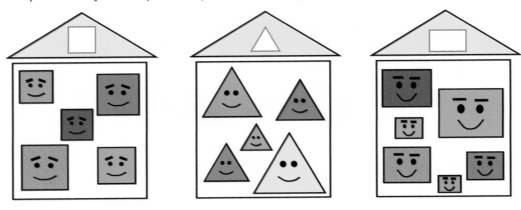

LEARNING OUTCOMES

Children can use geometric shape as the basis for sorting triangles, squares and rectangles in a variety of colours and sizes into three groups.

Once children acquire the concept of sensory standards, they no longer require 2D or 3D sensory standards to help them identify an object's shape. However, they will continue to use their fingers to help them to compare standard and object in some cases. In this situation, the hand is not the organ of perception but it helps the eye to follow the contour of the object.

The action of perceptual modelling

Children analyse complex objects that consist of more than one sensory standard. The child looks at the whole object, divides it into separate parts according to the relevant sensory standards, identifies its relationships, imagines an internal model of the whole object and then assembles all the elements in order to produce an image.

ACTION OF PERCEPTUAL MODELLING

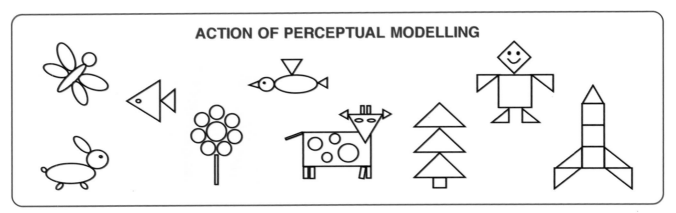

CATERPILLARS   **SENSORY MATHS - 42**

GEOMETRIC COLLAGE

AIMS

- To develop perceptual modelling (visual analysis of an object with several components: visualisation of geometric shapes that can substitute for the components and synthesis of the object from the geometric shapes).
- To develop analytical skills – break down a complex object into its component parts.
- To develop synthetic skills – recreate a complex shape from component parts.

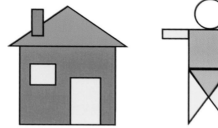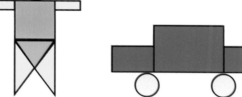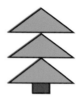

LEARNING OUTCOMES

Children create collages using geometric shapes.

CREATIVE MODELLING

Through Creative Modelling we are able to teach children how to create representations of aspects of the real world; and in this process we help them to develop mental models of the realities they learn to represent and emotional responses to them.
Galina Uradovskyh

This programme introduces young children to a range of carefully structured activities with an unusually rich educational content. The sessions address every aspect of the Foundation Stage areas of learning.

Perceptual modelling and the creation of thematic images

At the heart of each session is a practical application of sensory mathematics. We analyse compare and select mathematical shapes in a variety of colours and then synthesise the shapes to create representational images based on one of a number of recurring themes – woodland, orchard, meadow, town, street, decorative objects, animal forms and celebrations.

Understanding transformation

At the heart of each session is the creation of a representational image based on one of a number of the themes outlined above.

Each session involves the transformation of an original image based on one of the themes. The transformation might reflect a natural process (seasonal change), a natural form (completing the incomplete image of a plant or animal) or a human activity (making decorative or functional patterns, celebrating). Working with a teacher, young children create compositions across some of the most important genres of representational art; urban and rural landscapes, still life, representations of functional and decorative objects, and of animals.

Scaffolding symbolic and artistic expression

The materials developed for the programme enable young children to "stand a head taller than their current selves" in the creation of satisfying representational images. They pare down the process of creating representational images to the most essential building blocks. Consequently it is very easy for young children – and their less artistically inclined teachers! – to satisfy the desire to create credible representational images long before they have developed the fine motor control needed for the skilled

manipulation of the tools of the artist's trade. With the most difficult technical elements of the task well supported, young children are able to concentrate on mastering those elements of the task that are within their grasp. These elements include such basics as identifying shapes and colours, using lines and dots, using all the space, and grasping symmetry and pattern.

Crucially, they also include developing a personal response to the subject of the composition.

Early success boosts self-confidence and self-esteem. These in turn inspire the continuing interest and participation that will, in time, lead to independent mastery.

However, Creative Modelling does more than allow children to represent their environment and express a personal response to it. It also:

- Provides children with a chance to develop the social skills required for group work.
- Allows children to learn from each other.
- Helps children analyse and understand their environment, teaching a number of cognitive skills. These include learning how to identify features of geometric shapes (colour and size); how to use the shapes symbolically, as substitutes for real objects or parts of real objects in representational images; and how to choose and organise substitutes to create representations of ever more complex objects.

- Helps children extend their knowledge and understanding of the world as they use talk, role play, song, dance and the creation of representations to explore the various themes that run through the programme.

Through Creative Modelling we are able to teach children how to create representations of aspects of the real world; and in the process we help them to develop mental models of the realities they learn to represent and emotional responses to them.

How is it done?

These sessions are built on the use of felt in a variety of colours. For each session you will need at least one large felt rectangle in a colour chosen to help suggest the theme of the session, e.g. blue for summer/early autumn, gold or yellow for late autumn, greys and cold blues for winter, black for night time.

You will need felt shapes to represent natural forms – specifically a way of representing the sun, a way of representing deciduous trees, fir trees, apple trees and branches, a way of representing grass and flower stalks, a way of representing icicles. In addition you will need a supply of geometric shapes in a variety of sizes and colours.

The "stickability" of the felt means that felt shapes placed on a felt background stay put when the children work with the material at a table; they even resist falling off if you mount the felt background on a wall for display. Yet the pieces can be moved, arranged and rearranged freely, so it's easy to change your mind about what you have done – the material itself supports reflection and improvement.

What is more, the felt feels nice to the touch. Placing the pieces provides a soothing tactile pleasure that encourages persistence and participation.

Once you have the shapes you need, it should be relatively simple to prepare the session backgrounds using the descriptions and illustrations provided in the notes for the sessions.

What written notes and illustrations cannot convey is just how satisfying, straightforward and effective this medium is in allowing and supporting artistic expression. Starting with very simple bold building blocks teacher and pupils alike are free to create an extraordinary range of striking and impressive representational images. Because the material is so easy to use – and because the tasks the children are asked to complete are so finely graded and achievable – the programme supports very young artists in creating work that would otherwise remain beyond their capabilities.

The expected outcome of helping children to acquire sensory standards through these processes of identification, comparison and perceptive modelling is that children will both internalise the standards and be able to use the procedures to allow them to analyse objects in their heads.

MATHEMATICS

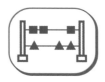

What is most distinctive about the Key to Learning approach is the use of visual models to allow children to see "at a glance" the most basic but also the most fundamental mathematical relationships. Judy Holder

Understanding numbers and the comparison of quantities

Most pre-school children learn to recite numbers, to count a small number of objects correctly and to recognise figures. And yet many of those same children have difficulties starting Mathematics at school. They follow the rules without understanding them.

For these children actions with numbers are some kind of witchcraft. If you are lucky your actions will lead to an answer that coincides with the one the teacher expects. Sadly, it comes as no surprise to learn that there are some primary school children who solve problems by adding numbers from the text of the problem to the page number.

Generally speaking, difficulties are not the result of poor counting skills, but a consequence of not understanding the most basic (but also the most fundamental) mathematical relationships. It is important not just to teach young children to count but to help them develop an understanding of what *number* is, to help them develop an understanding of the reality hidden behind the number labels and the counting procedure. And that is why – contrary to all intuition perhaps – we need to start not with number labels and counting but with the relationships themselves.

A number is not a label/symbol but a relationship between an idea (the unit of quantification/measure) and an object (what is quantified/measured). For example, the number of things in a group depends on your unit of measurement. When we look at a group of butterflies, we might count 3 butterflies or 6 wings. Similarly, when we need to measure the volume of water in a jug the answer we get (3, or 6, or 24) depends on the measure we choose (3 bottles full, or 6 cups full or 24 tablespoons.....) There must be a correspondence between the number we count and whatever it is we intend to measure.

If we can help children to understand this we will lay a secure foundation for later mathematical development.

Of course in this case, as in many other cases, you cannot just pour the required understanding into the child's head. Simply explaining what a number is will not help. Many adults – even those with a confident and competent but unspoken understanding – would struggle to put their understanding into words. Children can only develop and assimilate a secure understanding of fundamental mathematical relationships as a result of practical activity and discussion aimed at helping them to achieve this.

The Mathematics programme uses visual models and external mediators to provide activities that allow young children to "see" the hidden and invisible relationships for themselves.

Sensory Mathematics – laying the first foundations

Before children are ready to embark on the process of understanding precise quantification, they need to develop an understanding of the properties of physical objects that they will later quantify.

The Sensory Mathematics programme helps young children to analyse and internalise ideas about the physical properties of objects with the help of the sensory standards of colour, shape and size.

It methodically introduces children to the different characteristics of objects and provides kinaesthetic procedures to facilitate internalisation of the features of geometric shapes together with visual strategies for the systematic comparison of colours and sizes.

In the Mathematics programme children build on these foundations as they begin to quantify some of these properties more precisely.

The measurement of length, weight and volume

We measure volume, weight and length in conventional units that allow us to express our measurements precisely as numbers as well as to "compare at a distance" (for example, the amount of paint we need to paint a wall or the area of carpet required to cover a room).

The Sensory Mathematics programme introduces children to strategies for systematically comparing the size of objects. For example, children line objects up next to each other in a series reflecting size order and compare them visually. But they need to move beyond this. They need to develop the ability to quantify measurement and to grasp the idea of "comparison at a distance".

So, in Mathematics children use conventional measures such as a stick or a piece of string, using the whole of the measure repeatedly to measure a given object. They use such conventional measures to respond to scenarios in which they must compare objects that cannot be gathered together in one place.

For example, they might be asked to "go to the forest" to choose a Christmas tree that fits a particular room. This provides a rationale for the use of the conventional measure (it is far too costly and wasteful to cut down and transport a tree if we are not sure it will fit). The stick or the piece of string also provides the unit of measurement (a space that is two string lengths high requires a tree that is two string lengths tall – three is too big for the space, and one not big enough).

Maths "at a glance"

What is most distinctive about the approach is the use of visual models to allow children to see "at a glance" the most basic but also the most fundamental mathematical relationships. Finely graded practical activities involving a wide variety of visual mediators (pictures of objects, symbols, correspondence grids, tokens, abacuses and number lines) allow the children first to grasp and later to internalise these visual models.

For example, the children may compare two groups of objects; say 4 rabbits and 5 carrots. The children solve the problem of whether or not there are "as many rabbits as carrots" by superimposing images of carrots on images of rabbits, or by placing them side by side.

The children need to grasp the meaning of less than, more than and equal to, and to develop the ability to create equivalence in two ways, either by adding the one that is missing, or by removing the additional one. They do this by lining up the two rows of objects that obviously go together (carrots and rabbits) and comparing the resulting rows visually. The aligned rows now provide a visual model of the problem and its solution. The precise number of objects is immaterial at this stage, since if the objects are properly aligned, it is easy to see which of the two rows is longer.

The next step involves the use of tokens instead of images of objects.

At first the tokens provide some support for the children's visual thinking because they are selected to resemble the objects that are the focus for the comparison (orange tokens for carrots, brown tokens for rabbits; round tokens to find out if there are as many buttons as buttonholes, square tokens to compare the number of books to the number of readers). Later they use tokens with no visual resemblance to any features of the objects they are thinking about.

If the children work with 2 rows of objects (4 butterflies and 3 flowers) and they spread out the flowers so that they occupy more physical space than the butterflies, children may believe that there are more butterflies because they "see" a longer row. It is very important to help children to understand that number does not depend on the size of the object or the space over which a number of objects have been spread. Careful and systematic practice allows them to work out for themselves that the only way to change the number of

objects is by adding more or taking some away. In practice, this means we focus first on making sure children really understand what happens when we add one or take one away.

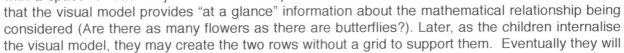

Finally the children compare by eye alone, using a visual mediator for checking only if required. Thus children may compare sets of classroom furniture ("as many chairs as tables"), using string to pair tables and chairs only if they have made a mistake and need a prompt to enable them to discover this for themselves.

In the early stages of the programme, the use of a grid, with a space for each object or counter helps to ensure that the visual model provides "at a glance" information about the mathematical relationship being considered (Are there as many flowers as there are butterflies?). Later, as the children internalise the visual model, they may create the two rows without a grid to support them. Eventually they will need to "look" at the two rows only with their "mind's eye".

At first the groups of objects for comparison will consist of items that all look the same. Gradually they encounter tasks which involve groups of objects that vary; they might compare a group consisting of dolls of different sizes and colours with a group consisting of an assortment of stuffed animals. The children need opportunities to practise with such groups to ensure that they learn to focus on the abstract process of comparison without being distracted by salient features of the objects themselves.

Axis lines, compound measures and counting by groups

An axis line is a universal mathematical tool with many applications. As a graphic model for the representation and comparison of quantity, it helps children compare quantities "at a glance", allowing them to identify which quantity is bigger and which smaller quite easily, without counting. Axis lines enable children to gain a deeper insight into fundamental concepts about measurement and number; and help lay the foundations for the future understanding of multiplication and division.

If we measure the same quantity using different measures, then the result changes. We get a different number at the end of our calculation even though the quantity we started with has not changed. What is more, the larger the unit of measurement the smaller the number of measures. For example, we can measure the same length with a long stick getting a small number of long stick lengths, or with a short stick, getting a larger number of short stick lengths; or we can measure in metres getting a small number of metres, or in centimetres, getting a much larger number of centimetres. We can use axis lines to record and compare the outcomes of measurement using different conventional measures: length, width, height, weight or capacity. They allow us to show children what happens when we measure a given quantity with different measures; the quantity does not change but the actual number of units we count varies depending on the measure we use.

Similarly, if we are counting a number of objects, our unit of measure is often one item, i.e. we count each separate object. However, we often count in groups of two or three objects. This is called a compound measure. With it counting by groups becomes possible. In fact, as adults we count in tens so automatically that we scarcely register that this is what we are doing.

We can use axis lines to help children gain deeper insights into the concept of number and to help lay the foundation for their future understanding of multiplication and division. For example, we can take a group of six small match boxes. Then use an arc (starting on the left at 0 and ending at 6) to mark six boxes. Divide the boxes into groups of two and record how many groups we have on an axis line in one colour; then divide them into groups of three and record the results on the same axis line, in a different colour. By doing this we have created a graphic model that allows the children to "see at a glance"

- how many of each type of group (groups of two, groups of three) we have
- that there can be different ways to split a quantity into equal groups
- that if we have more objects in each group, we have fewer groups

The graphic model and the procedures for creating it facilitate insight into counting by groups. The child can record the total number of groups of two or groups of three without having to count them and remember a total. The child can also compare and consider the results of counting in groups of two or groups of three without having to remember information about the actual numbers.

As Alex Kozulin puts it, "Children learn algebra first in order to organise their thinking processes."

Mathematics is a lively and accessible programme, involving the use of stories, scenarios, kinaesthetic procedures, visual prompts and games.

Quality not quantity

It is unwise to push children prematurely into working with big numbers. Ten is the ceiling for a four year old; five is plenty. What is really important is not quantity but quality – the quality of a child's understanding of quantity.

We recognise quality of understanding when we see:

- The ability to count objects attentively, sequentially and precisely, without missing an object, without counting the same object more than once; and without using incorrect number labels.
- The ability to determine the number of objects in a group by counting and then repeating the final number label to give the total.
- The ability to use counting to reach accurate and consistent conclusions about whether or not two groups of objects are equal or unequal in number.
- The ability to use the results of counting to compare groups of objects, in spite of such features as the size of the objects in the group, the nature of the objects, and the way the groups are arranged in space.
- The ability to recognise that every number in a number sequence is one more than the number before it, and one less than the number that comes after it.
- The ability to use this recognition to draw conclusions when comparing two groups (e.g. 4 pencils and 5 books means one more book than there are pencils).
- The ability to create equality between one group and another that contains one more object using two strategies; either adding an object to the smaller group or taking away an object from the larger group.
- The ability to create equality between one group and another that differ by more than one more object.
- The ability to recognise the digits that symbolise known numbers.

These secure number skills are the outcomes of a learning process that does not start with a focus on numbers and counting procedures, and that deliberately delays working with large numbers. Paradoxically, we need to remember that children who have learned to recite the numbers one to a hundred may be less of a cause for celebration than those who have spent an equal length of time learning to count to four successfully, reliably and consistently, and who really do understand that four is one more than three and one less than five.

LOGIC

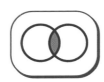

Children are not lone discoverers of Logical Rules but individuals who master their own psychological processes through tools offered by a given culture. Alex Kozulin

The Logic programme helps children to develop the ability to analyse objects and events, see their "invisible" sides, identify their most essential characteristics', think sequentially, draw conclusions, classify and systematize information.

Using Venn Diagrams and Classification Trees as well as substitute shapes to provide visual models of logical concepts, the programme offers a distinctive approach to the introduction of two basic logical processes; classification and seriation. It provides an early, coherent introduction to these mental processes in a developmentally appropriate, entertaining and accessible manner.

Making logical connections

The mental processes required for logical thought are vital but children will not just develop them spontaneously. Adults have no difficulty in classifying, in ordering objects according to the degree to which they possess a given characteristic and in understanding the implications of sequences. For example, if experience or prior knowledge tells us that a train moves more slowly than a plane but faster than a car, then we know we can assume a plane moves faster than both a train and a car.

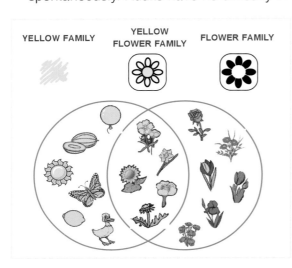

YELLOW FAMILY   YELLOW FLOWER FAMILY   FLOWER FAMILY

In contrast, young children may be able to tell us about a certain quality, for example that they are taller now than they were when they were babies. However they will not know how to organise objects by the degree to which they possess that quality, for example they will not be able to organise a group of children by increasing height.

Equally they have not yet grasped the idea that a general set must be bigger than the subsets included within it. Thus they may be able to tell us that tulips, roses and carnations are all flowers, and that wasps, bees and butterflies are all insects. But given a group containing many tulips and some roses they will probably not be able to answer the question, "Are there more flowers or more tulips?" They will see a lot of tulips and say: "More tulips."

Furthermore they do not realise that members of a subset have additional features which differentiate them from other members within a wider set. It may not be obvious to them that when sorting by colour a red triangle belongs in a set of red objects, rather than the set of blue objects which happens to include a blue triangle as one of its members.

As adults we make such connections and draw such conclusions so easily that we take the ability for granted. We do, but young children do not. This is not just lack of knowledge. Even where children have the prerequisite knowledge, they are unlikely to be able to put it to use, because they have not yet created a coherent mental framework within which to organise what they know. They do not yet grasp even the most obvious features of a classificatory system.

Making the intangible tangible

The Key to Learning Logic programme offers a distinctive approach to the introduction of two elements of logical thinking. It uses external mediators and visual models to introduce young children to basic principles of classification and seriation. Activities in this programme allow the children to analyse objects and events; to identify their essential characteristics and classify them; to think sequentially and to draw conclusions.

A highly significant feature of the curriculum is the structured introduction of simple Venn Diagrams and Classification Trees. Such diagrams, together with a variety of other visual prompts and external mediators, form the visual models which help young children to "see" logical concepts and connections without the need for many words.

The programme uses simple Venn Diagrams and Classification Trees as visual models to help children grasp classification. The visual impact of a large circle (the set) enclosing two or more smaller circles (the subsets) in and of itself forms an external mediator of the very powerful idea that useful classification is both systematic and hierarchic. The use of these diagrams, together with a variety of other visual prompts, helps young children to "see" without the need for many words that a set consists of objects with certain common characteristics; and that we can create subsets within a set by using additional specific features to differentiate between the subsets.

Seriation means organising members of a group by the degree to which they possess a specific quality, for example organising a group of children in height order. Here, the Key to Learning programme helps children to grasp the concept of seriation through the use of external mediators to create a visual model of the concept. The children use strips or circles of material that increase incrementally in size, visually embodying and externalising the "invisible" concept of an increasing or decreasing characteristic.

Of course, this visual modelling will make sense only if the child already has a rich repertoire of relevant experiences, ideas and vocabulary to draw on. There is no point in trying to arrange children in order of height before a child has a concept of height. And there is no point trying to classify animals if the child has no prior knowledge of them!

An ordered world view

The Logic programme allows young children to grasp logical concepts visually, and then to make use of those principles to solve problems. It helps them begin to create the coherent mental framework they will use in later life to organise what they know effectively.

The Logic programme helps young children develop the ability to think systematically about the world. They begin to discover the principles by which they can organise and classify the world around them. They begin to "see" those invisible attributes of objects and events which underpin an adult's perception of an orderly world; a world in which objects are not separate or randomly linked but rather systematically connected by their inherent characteristics.

CONSTRUCTION

To achieve the goal the children need to analyse the given problem; to generate solutions; to choose the correct blocks to implement their solutions; to be able to analyse the essential parts of the structure, selecting what is required and rejecting what is inessential; and to combine the different elements correctly to solve the constructive task. Nikolai Veraksa

Block play is routinely offered as an activity in preschool settings. It is an old favourite and its benefits seem so obvious that we rarely pause to question them. But perhaps we should.

Free block play predominates. We provide the blocks; the children manipulate them, squabble over them, and (if all goes well) create stable structures out of them. They may ascribe function to their structures; they may be able to describe them verbally; they may play with them along the lines suggested by the descriptions they have provided.

If we follow a more prescriptive approach we may provide the children with models to copy – possibly made out of blocks, but more commonly in the form of the pictures and diagrams that came packaged with the set of blocks when we purchased them.

Can we do better? What are the limitations of these conventional approaches?

Alexander Luria and the developmental potential of block play

The prominent Russian psychologist A. Luria described how our conventional approaches to block play may limit its rich developmental potential.

He noted that, generally speaking, Early Years practitioners adopt two approaches to block play. They provide pictures of building block structures for individual children to copy, or they encourage free play with the blocks either by suggesting ideas (build an airport, build a zoo) or by allowing the children completely free reign.

Luria pointed out that both approaches have limitations. Why did he make this claim? To answer that question we must define what we mean by constructive abilities.

What do we mean by constructive abilities?

Constructive abilities are a range of specific cognitive, self-regulative and communicative abilities that children can develop through block play:

- visualising and analysing structures in space
- verbalising and articulating their ideas to communicate their vision
- analysing the relationships between parts of a structure
- choosing blocks that are suitable for creating a structure
- choosing blocks to represent every part of a structure
- selecting the most appropriate blocks for this purpose
- using visual models as mediators to guide the construction process
- creating stable structures and constructing them skilfully
- learning to look at objects from different perspectives
- planning, discussing, creating and realising their own designs
- representing structures graphically
- using language to facilitate shared building activity

Luria proposed that to develop true constructive abilities block play must fulfil certain requirements:

- It must involve a predetermined structural challenge.
- It must embed the challenge within a compelling narrative that creates a goal that the child wishes to achieve.

The limitation of lonely copying

What are the limitations of an approach to block play that involves working on your own to copy a structure?

Child centred practitioners readily grasp the limitations of a prescriptive task. When we ask young children to reproduce a block structure, we do not challenge them to think about how to solve the construction problems involved for themselves. All the information is given; the child's role is limited to choosing the right blocks, mechanically, step by step; either the child can do it and the structure creates itself, or the child can't and gives up. In either case the child may benefit from the perceptual matching and the practice in hand eye co-ordination that the task involves. However, to qualify as a true developmental game or activity, a task must reach beyond drill and practice in perception, forming associations and developing manual skills. There must

also be a cognitive (intellectual and creative) challenge. Simply copying a structure lacks a true developmental focus. That is why on its own mechanical copying tasks become boring and, left to their own devices, children can rarely finish them.

Of course, this does not mean that we can never ask children to copy a model! To help to build the secure foundation upon which to build true constructive abilities we need to provide a sequential introduction to the blocks and their properties. Three year olds benefit from building by imitation and by copying examples, providing that we take care to make the activity meaningful through the use of exciting stories, social interaction, and dramatic dynamic presentation.

We must also remember that these activities are a first step and not an end in themselves. From the very beginning we must plan for progression, moving on as soon as the children are ready.

Free block play

It may be less obvious that free play sometimes provides an equally low level experience.

The most important feature differentiating free block play from building by imitation or by copying an example is that children have some bright and exciting goal in mind. This creates an image of an

end product, and the motivation to work towards realising it. But it does not provide the means of achieving it. The children must look for solutions themselves. They have to choose the building elements that can be used to solve the problem.

As they build, both the goal itself and the process by which it will be achieved remain fluid; both the details of the structure and the construction techniques emerge from the process itself. Consequently free constructive activity supports extended periods of focussed play; children can become engrossed in it.

Clearly free block play is an invaluable form of activity, and one to encourage. However, all is not quite as rosy as it could be.

The trouble with free block play

The difficulty with free block play is subtle.

For young children, free block play can take place in a symbolic space where the ordinary rules of physical space don't apply. Children can easily allocate any meaning they require to some object, and can easily change the meaning of the object according to the scenario in their heads. Consequently, they can easily avoid analysing the practical and objective properties of objects and materials. Constructive activity becomes play with substitute objects, e.g. this cylinder is a tree, this brick is a car, this cube is a dog, etc.

Even children who take part in free block play for extended periods are unlikely to develop true constructive abilities. Such play slides rapidly into a game useful for developing language and imagination but of minimal value for the development of constructive abilities.

This is because the symbolic world offers no practical constraints. **Naïve** construction tells a story about a visual idea but does not analyse it or physically embody it with any precision. Children do not have to analyse which constructive elements are useful for solving this or that task, which typical combinations will be good in this or that situation.

Naïve construction is also impulsive. Flitting from one goal to another, children do not plan. They do not take into account whether the materials available will create the structure they envision. They do not consider if the structures they imagine meet the purpose designated for them; nor do they check whether their finished structure has the objective properties required. They neglect the inherent physical properties of the blocks themselves.

The development of true constructive abilities

To be developmental, a game or activity has to reach beyond drilling, perception and forming concrete associations and move children on cognitively, i.e. it must help children to develop intellectual and creative abilities.

We have already noted Luria's two requirements for block play that will promote the development of constructive abilities:

- It must pose a predetermined structural challenge.
- It must embed the problem within a compelling narrative that creates a goal that the child wishes to achieve.

A task is goal directed when children have a specific and predetermined goal formulated either verbally by the teacher by the children themselves or in the form of a 2D or 3D model to copy. The goal imposes a set of constraints – the conditions of the building task. To achieve the goal

the children need to analyse the given problem; to generate solutions; to choose the correct blocks to implement their solutions; to be able to analyse the essential parts of the structure, selecting what is required and rejecting what is inessential; and to combine the different elements correctly to solve the constructive task.

These two features – a goal and an active search for a means of achieving it – are the hallmarks of truly developmental constructive activities. Consequently every activity in the programme relies on children "buying in" to a goal set by an absorbing story and having time allowed to satisfy the need for imaginative free play based around the structure and the narrative.

Crucially, however, the programmes also introduce a third feature to ensure the development of true constructive activities. This is a range of block play activities based on pioneering work by the Russian psychologist A. Mirenova; activities involving the use of "ghost models". Research by Russian psychologists involved in this work found that the benefits of this type of activity extended far beyond the context of block play; there were improvements in cognitive, self-regulative and communicative abilities.

Ghost Models

A "ghost model" is a model which conceals some aspects of the process required to produce (or reproduce!) it. The ghost model presents a 2D or 3D outline of a structure but no details of the blocks required to recreate it. The child's task is to work out for him/herself how to recreate the model. There is no ready to hand method available for solving the problem of recreating the ghost model from blocks. Each ghost model can be built in many different ways. There is one problem, but there are many solutions, and it is important to encourage children to develop as many different solutions as they can.

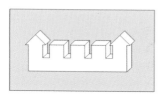   

Psychologically an approach involving ghost models differs very sharply both from copying and from free play. The given model immediately sets a predetermined goal, while the fact that there is no ready solution provides interest, often holding attention for an extended period.

How to solve the mystery of a Ghost Model

To solve the mystery of a ghost model, children must perform some or all of the following tasks:

- Look carefully at the given model
- Analyse it – visually deconstruct it into different component parts
- Imagine the components required to reconstruct it and try them out mentally
- Select the appropriate blocks
- Use them to reconstruct the spatial relationships between the component parts of the model
- Manipulate them skilfully to produce a stable structure
- Compare the reconstruction with the given model
- Evaluate the degree of correspondence between model and reconstruction

The advantages of Ghost Model activities

Ghost modelling promotes the development of visual thinking, analysis and constructive synthesis. Children have the opportunity to perceive basic geometric shapes, but this is not a passive perceptual activity. Children must stay actively engaged if they are to successfully analyse a visual model and identify its elements. In the process they gain an understanding of geometric relationships – both visually (as they look) and practically (as they build) which is not available to perception alone. Perception itself evolves.

Another important benefit of working with ghost models is that each one has many possible solutions; by encouraging children to search for several solutions we nurture creativity and flexible thinking.

Finally, the nature of ghost model type tasks helps to ensure that children remain actively engaged but grounded in practical reality. They must compare their solutions with the original and evaluate the degree to which they got it right. This is a self-checking exercise; the children are bound to notice even a slight departure from the size or shape of the original. This in itself makes it very much more difficult for children to slip into the realm of purely symbolic play.

Consequently, it becomes much easier to maintain interest while staying firmly within the domain of developmental constructive activity.

Construction activities and the development of mathematical concepts

A key feature of the Construction Programme is that it provides a wealth of mathematical content. The programme demands the use of a rich mathematical vocabulary in a practical, visual context. As they talk about their work the children have the opportunity to access mathematical vocabulary that includes the names of the building blocks and the 2-D shapes to which they correspond in plans; names for concepts such as edge, side, corner, face, flat, solid, straight, curved, plan, elevation, similar, different; for actions such as balance, build, connect, put together, take apart, stack, increase, decrease ; and for prepositions and prepositional phrases such as on top of, to the left of, to the right of, next to, under, above, behind, in front of, etc.

The children have opportunities to discuss how blocks, diagrams and constructions are similar to or differ from one another. They acquire a practical understanding of the physical properties of the blocks and their orientation. They develop a practical knowledge of relative length and width, including ideas about making things longer, shorter, taller, and wider, and ideas about multiples or fractions of blocks. This helps to lay the foundations for measurement. The programme provides a practical context for developing one to one correspondence, as the children compare one real block with another in a 3D model or with its representation in a 2D diagram. The children also encounter the earliest geometrical concepts, discovering symmetry, and becoming aware of pattern as a rhythmic sequential orientation of different blocks.

Visual-Spatial Modelling

Over the course of the Construction programme we help children to plan, execute and evaluate a range of constructions. In the early stages of the programme, the teacher's simple 3D models act as the visual tools that guide planning, analysis and evaluation of the structures they build.

Children learn to use 2D graphic representations of blocks and their relationships as substitutes for real structures. They encounter a range of 2D graphic models - their own drawings, detailed graphic models; outline graphic models ("ghost models") and schemes (generalised representations of objects and their relationships).

The stencils are external mediators that allow the children to link elements of a real 3D structure with their graphic representation. They are a tool to support children's analysis of a 3D structure; they also support self-regulation, helping young children to maintain and direct their focus and to control and manage their analytic and drawing activities.

The children use specially prepared block stencils. These have slots identical in size to different projections, i.e. front, top and side views, of each of the blocks. They use the stencils to create graphic representations of 3D structures. Later on, children can be introduced to block stencils which have scaled down slots. As the children learn to use these stencils, they free themselves from the preliminary reliance on one to one correspondence between the size of the block and the size of the graphic representation. They learn to represent and visualise any structure, regardless of its size or complexity.

Why do we introduce graphic models? It is because they are such a useful and significant cultural symbolic tool for thinking and planning. They are visual representations that can be seen with both our physical and our mind's eye. They can be remembered and referred to as an aid in organising thought. They help us select just those features of reality that are essential in solving a problem and guide us as we home in on them. As the Russian psychologist Olga Diachenko put it, "a child confident with visual modelling becomes capable of using models mentally. With their help he is able to process the information offered by adults, visualising the results of his actions in advance.

These are the qualities characteristic of a high level of development of cognitive abilities."

When we draw graphic models we provide ourselves with a visual externalised record of our ideas; we do not have to manipulate real objects but can visualise what we intend in advance of our actions; and we can then use the drawing to support and evaluate our actions when we try to realise our ideas.

Similarly when we "read" graphic models they help us to analyse and internalise ideas about objects and their relationships, and thus to guide and support us as we plan and execute actions.

The ability to use graphic models confidently and competently frees the child's imagination and creativity.

Overcoming egocentricity

One of the developmental challenges that young children encounter is the need to overcome spatial egocentricity, i.e. to begin to recognise that what you see depends on your perspective. Piaget recognised that young children (between the ages of 5 and 8) find it difficult to grasp that the object they can see in front of them may look very different to someone looking down at it from above, or from the side. They do not know instinctively that if their position changes their perception of a fixed object will also change. Consequently they find it hard to imagine what an object would look like if they move from one position to another while it stays still; and to imagine what it looks like from someone else's perspective.

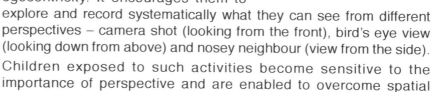

The Construction Programme, in its later stages, provides a structured, mediated approach to helping young children overcome spatial egocentricity. It encourages them to explore and record systematically what they can see from different perspectives – camera shot (looking from the front), bird's eye view (looking down from above) and nosey neighbour (view from the side).

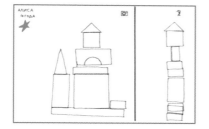

Children exposed to such activities become sensitive to the importance of perspective and are enabled to overcome spatial egocentricity much earlier.

Egocentricity may also refer to young children's difficulties in seeing social and emotional issues from any perspective other than their own. The programme also addresses these issues through an emphasis on sharing equipment and tidying up afterwards, group work, and the setting of problems with many possible solutions.

Construction activities and the development of self-regulation

Self-regulation requires the ability to plan and the ability to realise the plan.

One of the most important characteristics of successful adults is that they see themselves as architects of their own lives; they do not act on impulse alone, but are able to set themselves goals, make plans that will allow them to achieve those goals, and then execute those plans.

In much free block play action leads the idea. The Construction Programme supports the development of goal directed behaviour. We encourage children to generate and verbalise the ideas that will then lead their action.

Diagram – a visual model of a structure

The sessions in the Construction Programme develop children's ability to plan, to articulate what they have planned and to analyse the structure of objects and the relationships between their different parts. To do this they learn to use an important mental tool. This is a diagram which acts as a visual model of a structure that the children will build using a set of modular building blocks.

Modular blocks

Modular building blocks are blocks that have been designed so that the dimensions are interrelated. The basic unit is the cube. The other blocks are all multiples or a division of this unit, e.g. a brick is twice as long as a cube, one cube wide half a cube thick. Well made wooden blocks, with precise measurements, will reinforce mathematical concepts relating to measurement. It is easier to create stable structures with well made blocks, so they also help to keep frustration levels to a minimum.

Who and how often?

This programme can be used with children between the ages of 3 and 8. Differentiation is by the introduction of tasks of increasing complexity, matched to the children's developmental level, rather than their chronological ages.

The programme is most effective when it is delivered in one structured session of approximately 20-30 minutes per week, but with access to building blocks during self initiated play during the rest of the week to provide opportunities for consolidation.

The importance of flexibility

Do not feel obliged to move on quickly. Younger or less able groups may need more than one week to complete all the activities in a session; this is a matter for the teacher's judgement.

Similarly, it is important to maintain an open and flexible attitude towards the detail of the construction topics themselves. For example, when the children are working on boats and ships they may be interested in building pirate vessels. Let them. They may want to build a Batmobile instead of a car, or an alien space ship instead of a rocket. It is important to encourage children's initiative and to be willing to change the planned lesson to incorporate their ideas.

Keeping it real

During the Construction Programme we ask children to build 3D representations of real objects; houses, stairs, bridges, furniture, paths, ships, roads etc. To maximise learning and engagement, we need to help children develop an interest in the construction topics and knowledge of them before we ask them to build. This can be achieved by weaving the theme of a session into other planned activities, e.g. if the topic is bridges, the children could look out for bridges during a walk, read stories and information books featuring bridges during story time, look at pictures of bridges in books or on the computer etc.

Time for play

To ensure that the children find the Construction activities meaningful and memorable, we also need to ensure that they are deeply embedded in the world of play. We must allow plenty of time for the children to bring their constructions to life once they have finished building them. Supply the children with small world toys and let them play until they have exhausted all the possibilities (or you have run out of time!).

Types of construction methods

During the Construction Programme, teachers use different types of construction methods. These are: building by imitation (Copycat Step by Step and Copycat All at Once); building by copying a detailed 3D example (Twins – Concealed Construction); building from a 3D outline model (Ghost Model); building from a 2D graphic model (Camera Shot – front view, Bird's Eye View – top view, Nosey Neighbour – side view, Miniature – scaled down diagram, Ghost Outline Diagram and

Schema – schematic drawing); building to meet given criteria (Scenarios); building according to individual design (Individual Design) and building according to group design (Group Design). Detailed information about all of these methods can be found elsewhere in the programme.

Tidy up time

At the end of the session encourage the children to dismantle their structures and to sort all the building blocks into the correct trays, i.e. trays with picture cards corresponding to the shapes of different blocks. Make a game of it. For example, the teacher might close the session by explaining to the children that animals like to play with building blocks too. Each animal has a favourite: Frog likes cubes, Giraffe likes bricks, Bear likes cuboids, Hedgehog likes triangular prisms, and Elephant likes long boards... The teacher could put an animal in the correct tray, and then show the children how to give each animal its favourite blocks, demonstrating how to put the blocks away in the correct trays. This insistence on tidying up is partly because it provides practise in matching and sorting. However, a ritualised ending helps the children to delineate one activity from the next, facilitating the transition. It also helps children to become aware of themselves as part of a classroom community and reinforces the internalisation of classroom rules. Tidy up time is not time wasted; it is a valuable tool for the development of self-regulation.

The language of construction

Throughout the programme teachers need to use the relevant conceptual vocabulary. They need to introduce the names of the blocks and the language required to describe their features.

They need to use a rich mathematical vocabulary to describe the structures that can be built with the blocks. They need to use a rich vocabulary of verbs and prepositional phrases to describe building techniques and spatial relationships. However, the focus is not on getting children to learn to recite this vocabulary parrot fashion. The aim is for them to internalise the underlying conceptual content.

The children need to be supported in talking through their ideas about what they see and what they plan to do. It is important, particularly in the early stages, to accept the vocabulary the children use, while modelling the language they need to acquire.

Parallel Play and Shared Construction

The Construction Programme encourages two forms of group work: Parallel Play and Shared Construction.

In Parallel Play the children work individually to design and create structures connected by a common theme (e.g. ships in the harbour, rockets on a launch pad), giving the children a sense of being involved in a large scale activity. In Shared Construction the children work together as a group to plan and execute a large construction project. The key challenge is dividing and co-ordinating the various tasks.

The children must plan, negotiate their roles and tasks, share the equipment, complete the construction, and evaluate their work. To do this they must communicate effectively; they will need support and encouragement to talk through their ideas.

Setting out the ground rules

To avoid chaos and promote the development of co-operative and communicative skills, it is particularly important to teach basic rules for sharing, caring for each other and caring for the environment. Be prepared. Make time to set ground rules and to issue the following reminders:

- make sure you know what you have to do
- make sure everyone in your group has a job

- ask each other for things nicely
- give others what they ask for
- share with each other – only take the building blocks you need
- treat the blocks properly – handle carefully
- speak nicely and listen to each other
- help each other and help to tidy up.

Observation and Evaluation

The tasks we ask the children to attempt gradually become more complex over the course of the construction programme. Don't rush the children into building large structures prematurely – work with a few blocks on a small construction may look less impressive but yield deeper results.

We are looking for the development of the same set of underlying abilities over time. Consequently a set of straightforward questions should prove sufficient as a focus for observation of children and evaluation of their work and progress. For example:

- Does the child follow the appropriate sequence of steps in building the structure?
- Does the child stay on task long enough to finish building?
- Does the child build a successful "twin", i.e. a structure identical in size and shape to the model, using identical building blocks?
- Does the child compare her work with the model often enough?
- Does she compare the work carefully enough?
- How successful is the child at self correction?
- Does the child generate ideas?
- Does the child plan before she starts to build?
- Can the child articulate her plans?
- Does the child select the most appropriate blocks for her purpose?
- Does the child represent every part of a structure?

Similar observations can be used when the tasks become more complex, e.g. when instead of copying the teacher's 3D structure, the child uses a graphic representation (detailed or outline diagram).

Careful observation allows us to assess, but also to intervene. If we see that a child is struggling and making errors from which s/he is unlikely to be able to recover without help, we can use questions and other verbal prompts to help them sort out the difficulty.

Getting the most from the programme

Positive results from the Construction Programme depend on systematic and sequential work during prepared sessions. Positive results also depend on regular access to the blocks during self initiated play. Teachers are likely to notice a qualitative change during self-initiated block play, as children pick up on and extend the ideas they encountered during the formal sessions.

To mark the end of the Construction Programme, each child receives a certificate. This announces that the child is now a qualified Small World builder and architect. This is a celebration of the work the children have done. They have learned to plan, to articulate ideas, and to execute their ideas. Symbolically the certificates we give out do indeed represent our hopes and expectations for our young graduates; that we have prepared them to succeed not just in the Small World, but also in the real world that lies beyond it.

FROM THEORY TO PRACTICE
THE KEY TO LEARNING®
DEVELOPMENTAL CURRICULUM

According to Vygotsky, psychological development occurs through teaching/learning and upbringing using various types of spontaneous and specially organised interactions of the child with adults – interactions through which a human being assimilates the achievements of historically shaped culture. An essential role in this process is played by systems of signs and symbols.

Vasily Davydov

- SENSORY MATHEMATICS

- LOGIC

- MATHEMATICS

- STORY GRAMMAR

- DEVELOPMENTAL GAMES

- ARTOGRAPHICS

- VISUAL-SPATIAL

- CREATIVE MODELLING

- CONSTRUCTION

- EXPLORATION

- EXPRESSIVE MOVEMENT

- YOU – ME – WORLD

SENSORY MATHEMATICS

DEVELOPS THE ABILITY TO ANALYSE THE EXTERNAL,
VISUAL QUALITIES OF OBJECTS USING SENSORY STANDARDS
SUCH AS COLOUR, SHAPE AND SIZE. IT BUILDS THE FOUNDATION
FOR THE DEVELOPMENT OF MENTAL ABILITIES

Overview	Sensory Mathematics helps children to recognise and apply fundamental sensory standards of colour, shape and size. It enables them to begin to analyse objects and their relationships using culturally defined sensory norms.
	The natural world is almost overwhelmingly rich in its diversity of colours, shapes and forms. Our senses give us the ability to perceive this diversity, but it is culture that teaches us to understand our perceptions, for example, how to look and what to look at. Human cultures organise experience, systematising and classifying it in ways that allow us to make sense of the world and to operate confidently within it. Sensory abilities, shaped by our cultures, are the foundation upon which mental development builds.
Why are these skills important?	It is common to offer young children opportunities to name colours, or shapes, or to use size vocabulary. The Sensory Mathematics programme aims to do much more than merely teach young children to attach labels to objects – that is red, that is a triangle, that is big, that is small. Practical activities encourage children to consider what it means to say that something is red, or that this object is a triangle, or that one object is bigger than another. Tasks focus on how we can tell one colour or one shape from another; on how we know one thing is bigger than another, but smaller than something else. Naming the sensory properties of objects is the final consolidating step in a process of exploring and internalising perceptual concepts.
How does this programme work?	A particular feature of the programme is the very careful introduction of concepts of size. An object's shape and colour are intrinsic – they do not change unless the object itself changes. Size, however, is relative, and later conventional. A cat is small in comparison with an elephant, but big in comparison with a mouse – the object has not changed but the context has.
	Later stages of the programme introduce the children to some of the conventional systems we use for organising perception. For example, the children learn about the colours of the spectrum; about variations of geometric shapes (right angle, acute angle and obtuse angled triangles, rectangles with differing proportions of length and width); and about the different parameters of size (length, breadth and width).
The benefits of this programme	The programme embeds fundamental conceptual learning in carefully structured and sequenced everyday activities; games, stories, drawing, construction, role-play, etc. An important feature of the tasks is that they offer systematic procedures for developing understanding. These include a kinaesthetic procedure for exploring the properties of shapes, and an emphasis on systematic comparison in exploring colour and relative size.
	Another important feature is an emphasis on conveying that knowledge about sensory qualities is crucial. It has serious practical implications. Thus, for example, the children learn about colour by hiding mice from a dangerous cat, or about shape by feeding only appropriately shaped biscuits to each member of the shape family. There are good reasons to want to know!
	Last but not least, all the suggested activities have been tested in the classroom – and they are fun!

HIDE THE MOUSE

AIMS

- To develop colour recognition with reference to the seven colours of the spectrum: red, orange, yellow, green, blue, indigo, and violet.
- To practise matching colours to a sensory standard.

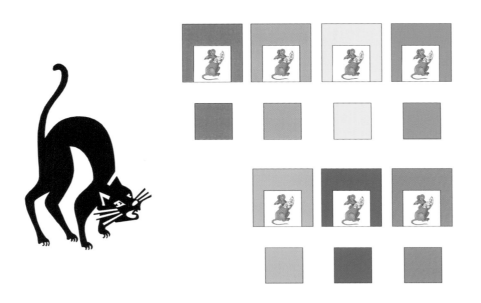

RESOURCES

For the teacher:

✓ Toy cat, finger puppet or cat picture;

✓ 7 mouse-in-a-house pictures in the 7 colours (20 x 15 cm);

✓ 7 doors in matching colours (9 x 9 cm).

For each child:

✓ 3 mouse-in-a-house pictures (10 x 8 cm);

✓ 7 doors in the colours of the spectrum (6 x 6 cm).

LEARNING OUTCOMES

- Children match doors to houses of the same colour.

- Children distinguish between the 7 colours of the spectrum when choosing the doors.

PROCEDURE

Once Upon a Time

■ Begin by telling a story to set the scene. Use pictures and/or puppets to help make the story vivid.

Once upon a time, there were some mice who lived in their own little houses at the edge of the field. Their village was called the Rainbow Mouse Village, and if I tell you the colours of their houses then you will understand why. One mouse lived in a red house, one mouse lived in an orange house, the next mouse lived in a yellow house, and then there was one who lived in a green house, one who lived in a blue house, one who lived in an indigo house, and one who lived in a violet house. So you see, their houses were painted the colours of the rainbow. Every morning the mice went out into the fields to get something to eat, and to play together. They were very happy, but they did have a problem. **A big problem!**

Close by the Rainbow Mouse Village there lived a fierce cat that liked nothing better than mouse for her breakfast. So when the mice went out to play, they always left the doors of their houses wide open. So if the cat ran after a mouse that mouse could just leap into its house and shut the door.

Can you see how the clever mice tricked the cat? Can you help the mice hide from the cat?

The cat is very fierce, but not that smart. The secret is, if the door is exactly the same colour as the house, the cat can't see the door and she will go away.

Help the mouse to find the door that matches its house. The mice will love you forever.

Hide the Mouse

■ Give each child three mouse-in-a-house pictures and seven doors. You are the cat and the children must save their mice from you. To do this they must "close the house doors to hide the mice" i.e. they must cover each mouse with a door that matches the colour of its house. The children need only match the colours correctly and should not yet be expected to name them – accept spontaneously offered correct colour names, but do not ask for them. If a child offers an incorrect name but selects the correct colour, use the correct name yourself, but don't labour the point.

■ Children may confuse colours, e.g. orange with yellow, indigo with violet. If a child does make a mistake whisper in his/her ear "I can see the door."

■ Encourage the children to play independently. Give each child a set of houses and doors to match. The number of houses will depend on how many you think individual children can cope with. Ask the children to "hide the mice from the cat." Again, as you go round the group you can encourage children to self correct by whispering, "I can see the door."

■ Next, make the task more difficult by setting tasks where some of the doors do not match any of the houses. Give the children a set of 3 houses and 7 doors and have them "hide the mice." Finally you may wish to give out all 7 doors and only one house. Ask the children to select the matching door for the house.

■ Once the children are familiar with the game they can play it out of session time.

Create Your Own Game

■ For additional practice, help the children create their own matching game to take home. Provide pictures of mouse houses, e.g. a red, green, and yellow house. Provide blank rectangles to be the doors. Ask the children to choose the appropriate colours to colour in the doors for their houses.

MAGIC SHAPE GLASSES

AIMS

- To recognise shapes using a reference shape.
- To look at objects from a novel abstract perspective .

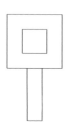  

RESOURCES

For the teacher:

✓ A set of square, circular and triangular objects;

✓ pictures of square, circular and triangular objects (You need enough to allow each child to name an example of each shape).

For each child:

✓ A set of Magic Shape Glasses, one for circles, one for triangles, one for squares.

LEARNING OUTCOMES

· Children recognise objects and pictures of object whose shapes correspond to a reference shape.

PROCEDURE

Magic Shape Glasses

- Show the children the three magic shape glasses (square, circular, triangular). Explain that if we look through the triangular glasses carefully it is easy to find objects and pictures of objects that have triangle shapes; we can find square objects through the square glasses and circular objects through the circle glasses.
- Show the children each magic shape glass and ask them to name the shape.
- Take one of the magic glasses e.g. the triangular one. Look at the set of objects through the glasses. Find the triangular objects and name them.
- Ask the children to look through the square magic glasses. Ask them to look for objects and pictures of objects that are also square.
- Ask each child in turn to name a square item. No one is allowed to name an object or picture that someone else has already named.
- Repeat using the triangle and the circle glasses.

BUILDERS AND ARCHITECTS

RESOURCES

For each pair of children:

✓ Houses – 3–5 rectangles, all the same height, with rectangular spaces cut out to represent doorways. The rectangular houses decrease in width by 0.5 cm successively; the width of the doorways decreases proportionally.

✓ Doors – 3 to 5 rectangles to fit the doorways.

✓ Roofs – 3 to 5 triangles. The base of each triangular roof matches the width of one house.

LEARNING OUTCOMES

· Children (builders) choose the right roofs and doors for the houses and place them correctly.

· Children (architects) check that roofs and doors have been placed correctly.

· Children work co-operatively in their designated roles.

AIMS

● To develop the concept of dimensions, e.g. width of an object.

● To develop the ability to estimate size visually, e.g. width.

● To develop the ability to work in a team, adopting a specified role.

PROCEDURE

Building a Town

■ The builders have not yet finished building the town. The houses are not ready. They have no doors and no roofs. Ask the children to help build the town. They need to find a door and a roof for each house and put them in the right places. The doors and roofs must fit perfectly, or the rain will get in.

■ Show the children a row of unfinished houses set out in decreasing order of size. Show them the roofs and doors arranged randomly. Demonstrate how to finish building the houses by picking out the doors and roofs required to complete each house. Put them in place, emphasising that each roof and door must match exactly and nothing must jut out.

■ Divide the children into pairs; one child is the architect and the other the builder. Give each pair of children a set of houses to finish, and the doors and roofs they will need for the job. The builder completes the houses by choosing and then putting in place the doors and roofs. The architect checks that the builder has done the job correctly. When the architect is satisfied that house has been completed correctly, s/he places it in the town (i.e. on the floor).

■ Admire the completed town, then have builders and architects change roles and build another.

■ The task can be simplified, e.g. provide fewer houses, provide houses with roofs attached, make the difference in width between the houses (and their doors) more obvious.

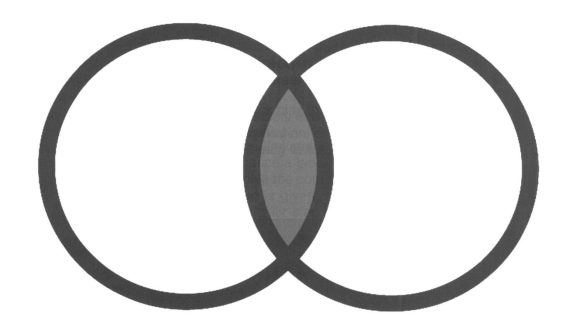

LOGIC

**DEVELOPS THE ABILITY TO ANALYSE OBJECTS AND EVENTS,
SEE THEIR INVISIBLE SIDES, IDENTIFY THEIR MOST ESSENTIAL
CHARACTERISTICS, THINK SEQUENTIALLY, DRAW CONCLUSIONS,
CLASSIFY AND SYSTEMATISE INFORMATION**

Overview

The Logic programme helps children develop the ability to analyse objects and events, see their "invisible" sides, identify their most essential characteristics, think sequentially, draw conclusions, classify and systematize information.

Using Grouping Circles, Classification Trees and Venn Diagrams as well as substitute shapes to provide visual models of logical concepts, the programme offers a distinctive approach to the introduction of two basic logical processes: classification and seriation. It provides an early, coherent introduction to these mental processes in a developmentally appropriate, entertaining and accessible manner.

Why are these skills important?

The mental processes required for logical thought are vital but children will not just develop them spontaneously. Adults have no difficulty in classifying, in ordering objects according to the degree to which they possess a given characteristic, and in understanding the implications of sequences. For example, if experience or prior knowledge tells us that a train moves more slowly than a plane but faster than a car, then we know we can assume a plane moves faster than both a train and a car.

We make such connections and draw such conclusions so easily that we take the ability for granted. We do, but young children do not.

They do not know that a general set must be bigger than the subsets included within it. Thus they may be able to tell us that tulips, roses and carnations are all flowers, and that wasps, bees and butterflies are all insects. But given a group containing many tulips and some roses they will probably not be able to answer the question, "Are there more flowers or more tulips?" They will see a lot of tulips, and say, "More tulips."

This is not just lack of knowledge. Even where children have the prerequisite knowledge, they are unlikely to be able to put it to use, because they have not yet created a coherent mental framework within which to organise what they know. They do not yet grasp even the most obvious features of a classificatory system.

How does this programme work?

The Key to Learning Logic programme offers a distinctive approach to the introduction of two elements of logical thinking: classification and seriation. What distinguishes the programme is the introduction of simple Grouping Circles, Classification Trees and Venn Diagrams. Such diagrams, together with a variety of other visual prompts and external mediators, are used as visual models which help young children to "see" logical concepts and connections without the need for many words. Activities in this programme allow the children to analyse objects and events, to identify their essential characteristics and classify them, to think sequentially, and to draw conclusions.

The benefits of this programme

The Logic programme allows young children to grasp logical concepts visually, and then to make use of those concepts to solve problems. It helps them begin to create the coherent mental framework they will use in later life to organise what they know effectively. They begin to develop the ability to think systematically about the world and to discover the principles by which they can organise and classify objects and events. They begin to "see" those invisible attributes of objects and events which underpin an adult's perception of an orderly world; a world in which objects are not separate or randomly linked but rather systematically connected by their inherent characteristics.

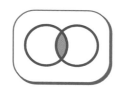

CLEVER QUESTIONS

AIMS

- To familiarise children with the objects that they will later quantify – analyse, describe and encode their properties.
- To practise identifying the properties of objects.
- To develop the ability to identify objects with similar properties.
- To practise using symbols to analyse the physical properties of objects (colour, shape, size).
- To introduce an active game to help children internalise the physical properties of objects.
- To promote a strategy for systematic, logical questioning.
- To introduce questions about different attributes of an object.
- To develop the ability to use a visual strategy to eliminate incorrect answers.
- To practise coding and decoding the physical properties of different objects.

RESOURCES

For the teacher:

✓ Magic bag.
✓ Set of attribute logic blocks.
✓ Attribute Symbol Cards.
✓ Hexagon card and 8 blank eliminating cards.
✓ 4 step Clever Questions Board – a board displaying information about the colour (red, blue, yellow), size (big/small), density (thick/thin) and shape of the logic blocks (circle, square, triangle, rectangle, hexagon).

LEARNING OUTCOMES

- Children can use symbols for physical properties (colour, shape, size, thickness) to identify objects correctly.
- Children ask questions systematically about different attributes of the logic blocks.
- Children can cover incorrect answers to questions on the Question Board.
- Children can use the information left uncovered on the Question Board to describe a hidden shape.
- Children can analyse, code and decode different properties of attribute logic blocks.

PROCEDURE

Library of Symbols

■ Place a collection of objects on the table and discuss their physical properties. Include objects that vary in shape, colour, size and thickness; include a group of objects that are obviously few, e.g. three toy goats, and a group of objects that are obviously many, e.g. a basket of pebbles or shells. Discuss the objects focussing on the physical properties or characteristics that help us distinguish between them. After the discussion put the objects out of sight.

- Spread a set of Attribute Symbol cards on the carpet. Tell the children that each card symbolises or stands for one thing that we could say about an object. Show them Attribute Symbol Cards representing colour. Ask if they can guess what each card stands for. Repeat for Attribute Symbol Cards representing shape. If the children find this difficult go systematically through all the colour and shape cards before attempting the more ambiguous symbols representing size and quantity.

- If they find the colour and shape cards easy, move quickly to guessing which Attribute Symbol represents big and which small, which represents thick and which thin, which wide and which narrow. Finally guess which Attribute Symbol represents one, which a few and which many.

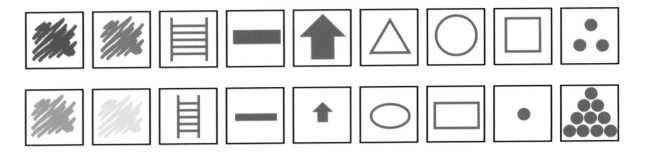

Clever Questions

- Hide a logic block in the magic bag. Ask the children, "What logic block is hiding in the magic bag?" The first time they play this game, encourage the children to guess the logic block, asking whatever questions occur to them.

- Now tell the children you can show them a better way to discover what is in the bag. Place the Question Board (with attribute symbols representing physical properties) where everyone can see it. Review what all the attribute symbols mean.

- Hide a shape in the magic bag. Point to the colour squares on the Question Board and say, "Let's find out about the colour first. Ask me, "Is it red?" "Is it blue?" or "Is it yellow?"

- If the answer to a question is "No", cover the square on the Question Board with a blank eliminating card. If the answer is "Yes", cover the remaining squares with an eliminating card, so that only the right answer is still showing. Repeat the process for size, density and shape.

- Only 4 pieces of information (one for each attribute) will now be showing. The child can now give a precise and detailed description of the hidden shape (e.g. It's the red, small, thin hexagon hiding in the bag).

- Take out the hidden shape for everyone to see. Repeat the game several times.

- Now let a child hide a logic block in the magic bag, answer the other children's questions and cover the eliminated symbols with a blank eliminating card.

Find the Logic Block

- Spread the attribute logic blocks on the floor. Place the four attribute symbol cards representing one of the logic blocks in a row on a tray.

- Ask the children to study the logic blocks carefully and choose the one that matches the attribute symbols.

- Repeat several times and then ask a child to choose the logic block and the attribute symbol cards that represent it. Have the child whisper the description to you, so that you can check that s/he has chosen the cards correctly before the rest of the group start to guess.

Four in a Row

- Spread the Attribute Symbol Cards on the floor. Choose one of the blocks and ask the children to choose the four Attribute Symbol Cards that represent the shape and put them on a tray in a row. Repeat several times.

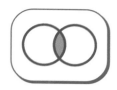

YELLOW FLOWERS

AIMS

- To build mathematical concepts of inclusion and exclusion.
- To introduce a Venn Diagram as a visual model of classification.
- To practise using a Venn Diagram to record differences and similarities between two sets of objects.
- To foster the ability to see the relationship between classes of objects
- To master the action of visual modelling.
- To develop the ability to use conventional symbols to represent a class of objects.
- To practise working co-operatively with others.

RESOURCES

For the teacher:

✓ 2 large hoops to form a Venn Diagram.

✓ Set of yellow objects and colourful flowers, including some yellow flowers (Alternatively use the picture cards provided).

✓ Corresponding Family Symbol Cards.

✓ Board or a large sheet of paper and an implement to draw with.

For each pair:

✓ A4 size Venn diagram.

✓ Set of Family Sort cards – yellow objects and colourful flowers, including some yellow flowers.

✓ Corresponding Family Symbol Cards and a Puppet.

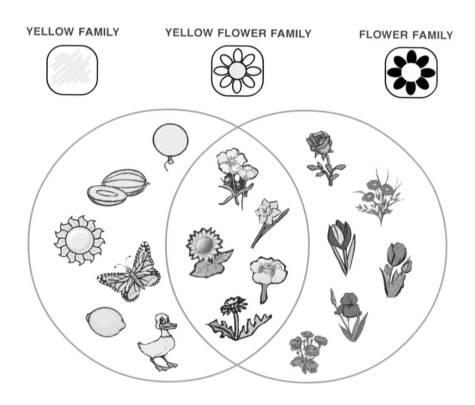

YELLOW FAMILY   YELLOW FLOWER FAMILY   FLOWER FAMILY

LEARNING OUTCOMES

- Children recognise symbol cards representing different sets.
- Children place flowers, yellow objects, and yellow flowers in the correct sections of a Venn Diagram.
- Children work together co-operatively.

PROCEDURE

- Place a variety of yellow objects, and colourful flowers on a tray. Some of the flowers should be yellow. Alternatively, use the picture cards provided.
- Place two large circles in front of the children. Explain that they are going to use the circles to help them sort the objects into two families – the Flower Family and the Yellow Family.
- Show the children a Flower Family Symbol (e.g. a stylised flower on some card) and place it in one of the circles. Explain that this shows us where the Flower Family goes. Repeat with a Yellow Family Symbol (a yellow card) for the second circle.

- Explain that everything in a circle must belong to the same family; only the flowers can go in the flower circle and only things that are yellow can go in the yellow circle.

Family Sort: Flower Family, Yellow Family, Yellow Flower Family

- Play "Family Sort." Show the children flowers or yellow objects and have them place the objects in the correct circles. If they make mistakes, prompt them by directing attention to the Family Symbol cards.
- After they have successfully sorted several objects, show them a yellow flower. If they do not spontaneously ask where this should go, draw attention to the fact that it belongs to both families – it can't really go with the Flower Family because the Yellow Family will be sad, and it can't go with the Yellow Family because the Flower Family will be sad.
- You may wish to discuss possible solutions to this dilemma before showing the children how to solve the problem by "making the two families overlap," i.e. overlapping the two circles to create a Venn Diagram with a space for yellow flowers between the two. Mark this space with a Yellow Flower Family symbol as a visual prompt (i.e. a card with a stylised flower on a yellow background).
- Continue with the game until you have sorted all the objects.

Independent Activity

- Give each pair of children an A4 Venn Diagram, a set of cards and a puppet. Ask the children to take turns "being" the puppet. The child without the puppet explains to the puppet where to put a card and why it goes there. The "puppet" places the card as directed.
- Continue until the children have sorted all their cards.
- Each pair then checks another pair's work.
- Swap roles and repeat if you have time.

You – Me – Us Venn Diagram

- Choose two children, a boy and a girl.
- Draw a Venn Diagram on the board or a large sheet of paper. Write the boy's name next to one circle, the girl's next to the other. Write "Both" next to the overlap.

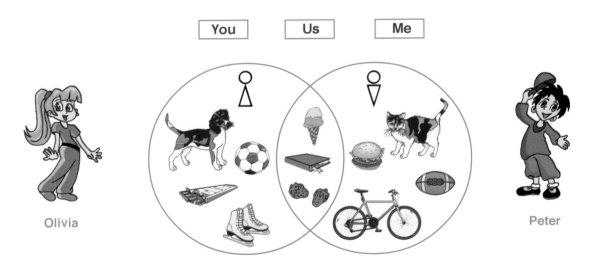

- Talk about the pair. You might include information about eye colour, hair length, clothing, food preferences, games they enjoy or dislike, sports they play, how they get to school, pets etc. Draw images or symbols representing what you discover about them in the correct sections of the Venn Diagram. Have children help you with the drawing, if possible.
- Display the Venn Diagram on the wall.

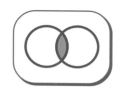

GROUPING CIRCLES

AIMS

- To enable children to use Grouping Circles to group objects
- To introduce the concept of a set – a group of objects with common characteristics
- To help children visualise the idea that sets can be divided into subsets
- To develop the ability to recognise members of a subset by their additional attribute
- To foster the ability to decode symbols
- To teach children to classify objects by two attributes

PROCEDURE

- Take the chosen geometric shapes (e.g. the triangles) out of the bag. Discuss the shape with the children. Remind them of times they have encountered the shape before and discuss the key features, e.g. all triangles have 3 straight sides.

- Ask the children if all the triangles are exactly the same. If necessary prompt them to tell you that the triangles are not identical, some are red and some blue. Ask the children to help you divide the triangles into two groups. Move the triangles as required to form two neat distinct groups within the original circle. Draw smaller circles around each of the subgroups.

- Help the children to consolidate their understanding of what they can now see by asking questions. Ask, "Which triangles are in one group

RESOURCES

For the teacher:

- ✓ Sets of 10 geometric shapes, e.g. triangles, circles, rectangles, squares.
- ✓ 5 of each in one colour and 5 in another e.g. 5 red and 5 blue triangles.
- ✓ Bag for the shapes.
- ✓ Large sheet of paper (A2).
- ✓ Two big Grouping Circles.
- ✓ Two small Grouping Circles.
- ✓ Shape and Colour symbol cards for labelling the Grouping Circles.
- ✓ Pair of Grouping Guides.

LEARNING OUTCOMES

- Children can use Grouping Circles to create sets and subsets of coloured shapes.
- Children can recognise and use Symbol Cards.

(the red ones) and which are in the other (the blue ones)?" Remind the children that they used a triangle symbol to show everyone that all the triangles belong in the large circle. Ask them if they can think of a way to show everyone which triangles belong in this small circle (pointing to either the red or the blue subset). Show how to mark the circle containing red triangles with a red blob, and the blue circle with a blue blob.

■ Tell the children that the shapes are very tired and need a rest. Take them out of the circle and put them in a bag. Tell the children that all the shapes have gone, but their mark has been left behind. It shows us where to put them next time they come out to play.

Help the Grouping Guides!

■ If the children help by pointing and saying, "Put this here", have the Grouping Guides ask, "How do you know?" If the children have difficulty explaining, use questions to prompt them. "What can you see that will help the Grouping Guides do their job?" If necessary, model the explanation: "The triangle symbol shows us where all of the triangles belong; the triangles are not all exactly the same; the red blob shows the red triangles where to go, the blue blob shows the blue ones."

■ Have Grouping Guides tell you where to put the shapes. Ask the children to watch in case the Guides make a mistake. Make some deliberate mistakes for the children to correct.

Shape Sort, Colour Sort

■ Ask the children to help the shapes find their places. The symbol cards should prompt them to sort the shapes correctly.

■ When they have sorted all the shapes, tell them that the shapes are very pleased because they are in the right places; all the circles are in their set, they are all in the same big circle; all the squares are in their set, they are in the other big circle. All the red squares are together in their small circle, all the blue squares are together in their small circle, all the red circles are together and all the blue circles are together.

Colour Sort, Shape Sort

■ Ask the children to turn round. Tell them the shapes are ready to come out again. Ask the children to help the shapes find their places. Do not draw attention to the changes.

■ Observe the children to see whether or not they can work out how to sort the shapes now that you have exchanged the positions of the Symbol Cards.

■ If the children have difficulties with this, prompt them, e.g. start with the set of red objects. Point to the red Grouping Circle. Remind the children that the red Symbol Card tells us that all the red shapes go in there. Point to the square Symbol Card and ask which shapes go there (red squares). Provide as much help as the children need to complete the task successfully.

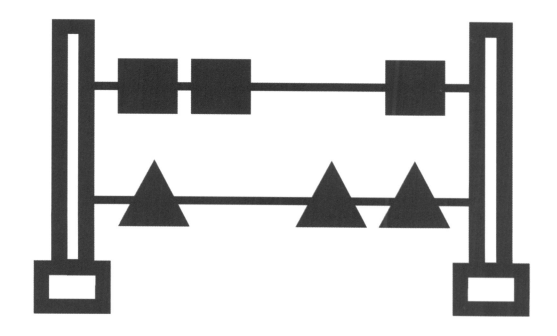

MATHEMATICS

USING VISUAL MODELS CHILDREN DISCOVER THE LANGUAGE
OF MATHEMATICS AND THE CONCEPT OF MEASUREMENT, COMPARE
DIFFERENT QUANTITIES AND QUALITIES OF OBJECTS AND EXPLORE
THE RELATIONSHIPS *MORE, LESS, EQUAL*

Overview

This programme introduces the concepts and language of mathematics and develops fundamental understanding of mathematical relationships. Children discover the concept of number; they learn to think about the relationship between what is being measured and the unit of measurement required for measuring it. The main task is to help children internalise concepts of relative quantity and relative size (length, weight, volume). We aim to develop the ability to make generalisations and to see connections through the use of visual mediators.

Why are these skills important?

Most adults accept the practical importance of mathematical skills, and in our eagerness for children to master them we are anxious to get on with the business of teaching children to count and solve number tasks. But should we begin with this? The result may be a classroom full of young children who can recite numbers up to 100, but cannot reliably count three bears. They may go through the rest of their schooling sometimes getting the right answers by following the rules, but fundamentally baffled.

A number is not a label or a digit, but the expression of a relationship between the unit of quantification and the objects or features quantified. When we look at a group of butterflies, we might count three butterflies or six wings. Similarly, when we measure the volume of water in a jug our answer depends on the measure we choose (24 tablespoons or 6 cups). By helping children grasp the underlying relationships, we help them to unlock the mystery of number.

How does this programme work?

What is most distinctive about the Mathematics programme is the use of visual models to allow children to see "at a glance" the most basic but also the most fundamental mathematical relationships; more than, less than, equal to. Similarly, they learn to understand and to use simple conventional measures (e.g. a stick) to respond to scenarios in which they must compare the size of objects that cannot be gathered together in one place.

Finely graded practical activities involving a wide variety of visual mediators (pictures of objects, symbols, correspondence grids, tokens, abacuses and number lines) allow the children first to grasp and later to internalise the mathematical relationships they model. At first tasks are concretely supported. For example, children discover if there are as many carrots in a field as there are hungry rabbits by superimposing images of carrots on images of rabbits.

Gradually the tasks require greater levels of abstraction, replacing images of objects with symbols and tokens, and direct manipulation of objects with simple graphs. Later still, as the children internalise the visual models, they practise solving problems by "looking" with their "mind's eye".

The benefits of this programme

What is really important is not quantity but quality – the quality of a child's understanding of quantity. The secure counting and measuring skills required to facilitate mathematical learning are the apparently paradoxical outcomes of a teaching and learning process that does not focus on teaching children to count. Instead children learn to understand what they need to count and how to count it.

Children develop insight into why quantification matters; insight into the use of measures for comparing weights, heights or volumes; and the ability to focus on exactly what it is that they are trying to measure when they quantify.

BUTTONS FOR BUTTONHOLES

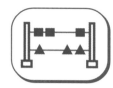

AIMS

- To develop the ability to use one-to-one correspondence to match two sets of objects exactly.
- To practise using tokens to facilitate one-to-one matching of sets of physically separated objects.
- To demonstrate the value of one-to-one correspondence in completing practical tasks.
- To foster the ability to participate co-operatively in role play.
- To develop the ability to select the required number of objects from a set.

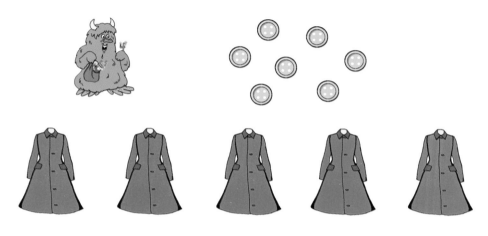

PROCEDURE

As Many Claps As...

- Stamp your foot once and ask the children to make as many claps as there were stamps. Repeat for different numbers of stamps and with different actions, e.g. winks, clicking fingers, clicks of the tongue. If you have time ask the children to take the lead, choosing an action, performing it a number of times, and asking the group to make as many claps as there were winks, stamps, etc...

Setting the Scene

- The focus of this session is on helping the children to practise and secure the ability to match objects exactly using one-to-one correspondence. Some children may already be learning to count; others may be learning to recite numbers without any grasp of the prerequisite underlying concepts. Consequently, if we want to ensure that the children are practising one-to-one matching, we need to inhibit counting.

- One way to do this is by introducing Greedy Gary the Number Guzzler. If you hear counting produce Greedy Gary. Explain that Greedy Gary loves to gobble numbers, and that if he hears anyone saying a number he will come to eat it. If you hear a child count, take Gary over to the child and whisper, "Greedy Gary has eaten your numbers, you can't use them."

RESOURCES

For the teacher:

✓ Greedy Gary, the Number Guzzler.

✓ Pictures of red coats with buttonholes.

✓ Cathy Counter (the doll who checks the children's work).

For each pair of children:

✓ Greedy Gary, the Number Guzzler.

✓ Box of buttons in a space designated as *The Button Shop*.

✓ Box of tokens (use plastic ones if possible).

✓ Carrying Box – a small box for transporting counters to *The Button Shop* and buttons back from it.

LEARNING OUTCOMES

- Children use tokens to help them match a set of buttons to a set of buttonholes.

- Children play the roles of shoppers and shopkeepers co-operatively.

- Introduce the scenario. Bring out Cathy Counter and tell the children that she is feeling very sad today. She ordered new coats for all the dolls online (over the Internet), but when the parcel with the coats arrived she saw there was a problem.

- Show the children a coat and ask if they can see what the problem might be. If necessary, prompt them to notice that there are buttonholes but no buttons on the coats.

- Tell the children they are going to help Cathy Counter solve her problem. Explain that there is a button shop in the classroom today and they are going to buy buttons from the button shop.

Modelling the Activity

- Ask the children if they know how to buy exactly the right numbers of buttons – but without any counting. Listen to their ideas.

- Show them the procedure you want them to follow. Produce the box of tokens, and take tokens out of it one by one. Match each token to a buttonhole. As you do so say, "As many tokens as there are buttonholes". Encourage the children to recite the phrase with you – rehearsing the phrase will help them to manage the activity by themselves today, and internalising it will help them remember how to do it tomorrow.

- Put the tokens in the "carrying box" and go to the shop. Explain that now you are the shopkeeper and you will show them what the shopkeeper does. Take the tokens out of the carrying box and lay them on a flat surface in the button shop. Take buttons out of a button box, one at a time. Match each button to a token. As you do so say, "As many buttons as there are tokens." Encourage the children to recite the phrase with you. Put the buttons into the now empty carrying box, take it to the coat, put a button on each buttonhole and show the children that you now have "as many buttons as there are buttonholes."

- Return the tokens and buttons to their boxes.

Shopping for Buttons

- Split the children into pairs. One is the shopper, one the shopkeeper. Send the shopkeepers to the button shop.

- Give each shopper a coat, a carrying box and a box of tokens. Ask the shoppers to take out "as many tokens as there are buttonholes." You can control the difficulty of the task by choosing coats with smaller or larger numbers of buttonholes. Have Cathy Counter come round to check that the children have taken the right number of tokens. If someone has made a mistake, prompt the child to correct the error by saying, "Cathy thinks you have some tokens left over" or "Cathy thinks there isn't a token for every buttonhole."

- When the shoppers are ready have them put their tokens in the carrying box ready to go to the button shop. Close the lids of the token boxes and put them out of reach. Note that putting away the token boxes and using a carrying box instead means that the shoppers have to plan how many tokens to use rather than just taking out what they need when they get to the button shop.

- Tell the shoppers that when they get to the button shop they must take out the tokens, and ask the shopkeeper for "as many buttons as there are tokens." The shopkeepers now match buttons to tokens and put the required number of buttons in the carrying box.

- The shoppers take the buttons back to the coats, put them on buttonholes and show Cathy Counter that they have in fact brought back "as many buttons as there are buttonholes". Cathy Counter helps the shoppers recognise and correct any errors before thanking the children for their help. Swap shoppers and shopkeepers and repeat the game.

FLOWER FOR EVERY BUTTERFLY

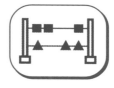

AIMS

- To confirm the ability to use external mediators (tokens) to identify and select a required number of objects.
- To confirm the ability to use tokens to facilitate one-to-one matching of sets of objects that are physically distant from each other.
- To develop the ability to use one-to-one correspondence to match two sets of objects exactly.
- To practise selecting the required number of objects from a bigger quantity.
- To develop the ability to create a visual model of the mathematical relationship between two sets of objects.
- To foster understanding of the concepts less than, more than and equal to.
- To demonstrate the value of one-to-one correspondence in facilitating the successful completion of practical tasks.
- To promote the development of co-operation and teamwork.

RESOURCES

For the teacher:
- ✓ Greedy Gary the Number Guzzler.
- ✓ Happy and Sad tokens.
- ✓ Correspondence Grid for Butterflies and Flowers.
- ✓ Correspondence Grid for Happy Faces and Sad Faces.
- ✓ 6 A4 cards with butterflies and 6 A4 cards with flowers.
- ✓ Red round tokens for flowers and blue square tokens for butterflies.

For a pair of children:
- ✓ Inspector's Glasses.
- ✓ Correspondence Grid for Butterflies and Flowers.
- ✓ Glue stick (optional).
- ✓ Two boxes of tokens: one with red round tokens for flowers and one with blue square tokens for butterflies.

LEARNING OUTCOMES

- · Children can match tokens to butterflies and to flowers.
- · Children show the quantitative relationship between the group of butterflies and the group of flowers by sticking tokens on a Paired Squares Correspondence Grid correctly. →

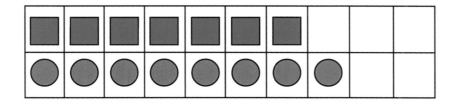

PROCEDURE

Group Activity

■ Bring out Greedy Gary the Number Guzzler and remind the children that if they count he will come and eat up all the numbers, so there must be no counting.

Children can place a happy face on the grid if there is a flower for every butterfly, and a sad face if there is not.

Children can use their own facial expressions to show whether there were more happy or more sad faces on the Sad or Happy Grid.

Children work together co-operatively.

■ Put out a sheet with images of some flowers in a corner of the classroom. Put a sheet with images of some butterflies on the table in front of the children. There should be one more flower than there are butterflies.

■ Tell the children a story about Butterflies and Flowers:

"There are some lovely wildflowers growing in the meadow over the river. Many wildflowers. There are also some lovely butterflies flying over here in the forest. Many butterflies. The butterflies know that there are wildflowers in the meadow and they want to taste some delicious nectar. But they do not know if there is a flower for every butterfly. They don't want to go until they are sure that all the butterflies can find a flower, because they don't want anyone to feel sad."

■ Ask the children if they can help the butterflies. Allow a brief discussion; explain that we can't pick the flowers and bring them to the butterflies, because if we pick the flowers they will die and they won't make any more delicious nectar.

■ Show the children how to help the butterflies find out if there is a flower for everyone. Choose a child, give him/her a box of round red tokens and ask him/her to go across the river and put a token on top of every flower, so that all the flowers are covered. Then the child must close the box and return across the river with the tokens in his/her hand.

■ Put a Paired Squares Correspondence Grid on the table. Ask the child to put the flower tokens on the lower row, one token to a space.

■ Choose a different child; give him/her a box of square blue tokens. Ask the child to put a token on top of every butterfly so that all the butterflies are covered, then to close the box and put the butterfly tokens on the upper row of the Paired Squares Correspondence Grid, one token to a space.

■ When the grid is complete, point to it and ask, "Which is more and which is less? Are there more butterflies or are there more flowers? Is there a butterfly for every flower?" Agree that every butterfly does indeed have a flower, that none of the butterflies are going to be sad, and that there is one more flower than there are butterflies.

Pair Work

■ Give each pair of children two sheets, one with flowers, one with butterflies. The two sets of images are always unequal, with a difference of one between them (either one more butterfly than there are flowers or one fewer). Ask the children to find out whether or not the butterflies will be sad; whether there is a flower for every butterfly.

■ Give one child a box of round red tokens for covering flowers, and the other a box of square blue tokens for covering butterflies. The children also need a Paired Squares Correspondence Grid and a pair of Inspector's Glasses.

■ The child with the red flower tokens places a token on each flower then shuts the box of flower tokens. His/her partner puts on the Inspector's Glasses and checks that each flower has a token. Then the first child transfers the flower tokens to the bottom row of the

Paired Squares Correspondence Grid, one to a space. (You may wish to have the children stick the tokens on a blank Paired Squares Correspondence Grid for a display or for their folders of work).

■ The child with the box of blue butterfly tokens now places a blue token on each butterfly, and then shuts the box of butterfly tokens. His/her partner puts on the Inspector's Glasses and checks that each butterfly has a token. Then the first child transfers the butterfly tokens to the top row of the Paired Squares Correspondence Grid, one to a space.

■ The pair must now decide whether there is a flower for every butterfly (making the butterflies happy), or one butterfly with no flower (making the butterflies sad). They choose a happy or a sad token and put it on the bottom right hand corner of the grid: a happy face if there is a flower for every butterfly, a sad face if there is not.

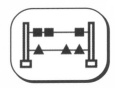

RESOURCES

For the teacher:

✓ Long strip of white paper 5 x 60 cm – the "roll of cloth".

✓ Green rectangle, 5x10cm – "the shirt".

✓ Yellow rectangle, 5x20cm – "the dress".

✓ Pencil for marking out the material.

✓ Pair of "dressmaker"s glasses'.

✓ Teddy Tailor.

For each child:

✓ Long strip of white paper 3x16 cm – "the roll of cloth".

✓ Abacus with 2 rows of beads in 2 colours.

✓ Green rectangle, 3x4 cm – "the shirt".

✓ Yellow rectangle, 3x8 cm – "the dress".

✓ Pencil for marking out the material.

✓ Pair of dressmaker's glasses.

DRESSES OR SHIRTS?

AIMS

● To develop the concept of number as a relationship between what is measured and the unit of measurement.

● To introduce the idea that units of measure are conventional.

● To foster the acquisition of practical measuring skills.

● To practise measuring the same piece of material using two different conventional measures.

● To introduce an abacus as a visual model for recording and comparing data.

● To introduce an abacus as a visual model of a quantitative relationship.

● To practise using an abacus to compare the quantities obtained when using different measures.

● To develop understanding of the concepts less than, fewer than, more than and equal to.

PROCEDURE

Setting the Scene

■ Talk to the children about their clothes. Talk about shirts, dresses, the materials they are made of, "rolls of cloth" etc. You may wish to use visual aids, e.g. pictures.

■ Look at an item of doll's clothing, e.g. a dress, and a similar item of child's clothing. Ask, "Which is more and which is less, is there more material to make the doll's dress or the child's?"

■ Repeat with a shirt and a dress – make sure that the dress very obviously requires more material than the shirt. Agree that we need more material for a dress.

Introducing Teddy Tailor

- Produce Teddy Tailor. Explain that Teddy Tailor has a tailor's shop where the teddies make dresses and shirts out of rolls of cloth. Show the "roll of cloth" (i.e. the long strip of paper) and explain that this is the roll of cloth that Teddy is going to use today.

- Explain that Teddy Tailor cuts the cloth into pieces and then makes each piece he cuts into either a dress or a shirt. Today Teddy wants to make whichever he can make the most, dresses or shirts. However, he has a problem. He doesn't know which is more and which is fewer – the dresses he can make from the roll of cloth, or the shirts. Ask the children to help him find out.

Model the Activity

- Show the children the teacher's green and yellow rectangles. Explain that one of the rectangles shows us enough cloth to make a dress, and the other enough cloth to make a shirt. We can use one to measure the dresses, and the other to measure the shirts.

- Discuss which measure is for a dress and which for a shirt. If they have difficulty remind them of earlier discussions.

- Put on the "dressmaker's glasses". Show the children how to measure "the roll of cloth" and record the measurements on the abacus.

- Describe and demonstrate each step carefully. Use either the shirt measure or the dress measure first; complete the measurement, then turn over the roll of cloth and use the other measure.

- Emphasise: placing the measure exactly at one end of the roll of cloth when you start; drawing along the edge of the measure to show where the measure finishes; using the pencil line to show you where to put the measure next.

- Show the children how to record the measurements on the abacus. Emphasise one row for dresses, the other for shirts; moving a coloured bead on the abacus from one side of the row to the other every time you place the measure on the "roll of cloth".

- When the measuring is complete look at the two rows on the abacus. Ask the children to tell Teddy Tailor "Which is more and which is fewer, the number of dresses or the number of shirts?" (Dresses are fewer,

LEARNING OUTCOMES

- Children can measure the same "roll of cloth" using two different measures.

- Children can say which measure they use for dresses and which for shirts.

- Children can use an abacus to record the number of times a "dress" or a "shirt" measure fits onto a "roll of cloth."

- Children can say that the rows of beads show more shirts and fewer dresses.

shirts are more). Have Teddy Tailor ask the children how they know ("We can see because the row of dress beads is longer than the row of shirt beads").

Individual Work

- Give each child a "roll of cloth", a pair of dressmaker's glasses, a pencil, measures for a dress and a shirt, and an abacus.

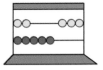

- Ask them to put on the dressmaker's glasses and use the measures to find out *which is more and which is less, the number of dresses or the number of shirts.*

STORY GRAMMAR®

**DEVELOPS A LOVE OF STORY, OWNERSHIP OF STORY LANGUAGE
AND A PROFOUND UNDERSTANDING OF STORY STRUCTURE
BY FOLLOWING A SPECIFIC SET OF PROCEDURES KNOWN
AS VISUAL MODELLING**

Overview

The Story Grammar® programme follows a specific set of procedures (Visual-Spatial Modelling) for helping young children develop a love of story, ownership of story language and a profound understanding of story structure.

Why are these skills important?

All young children like to listen to fairy tales, but do they really understand them? Or are they just responding to the adult reading or telling the tale? Sometimes what we read is interesting but incomprehensible for the children. We need to be sure that the children are, in fact, following the story. If you tell stories often enough then gradually understanding will come. But is it possible to speed up this process? Let's see!

How does this programme work?

Learning to retell the story is a gradual process. How do we facilitate it? How do we help children to master Story Grammar? We start by providing a rich emotional experience of the story to ensure that the storyline becomes apparent to the children. We develop children's deliberate attention when they are listening to a story. But how do we know that the children are listening? They may seem to be listening but how can we be sure that they are not thinking of something else? Maybe they are indeed listening to the story but are we sure they can identify the key events?

The essence of retelling the story is to be able to hold in mind its structure; in fairy tales events very often repeat themselves within this structure. Then we use a very effective process called visual-spatial modelling for helping young children to understand the content and sequence of events in a story (the actions) and to identify the relationships between characters. In visual modelling, we substitute one group of objects (tangible geometric forms) for another group of objects (real objects) and help children to create a mental link between the real object and the geometric form. This allows young children to hold in their hands the objects and characters that appear in a story – objects that are, in fact, imaginary and intangible.

Visual-Spatial Modelling is a complex process because children are using a spatial sequence to represent a temporal sequence. This activity is of particular benefit in developing abstract thinking skills. It helps to analyse essential events in a story. Children create a visual model of the story and then use the model to help them remember and retell it as independently as possible.

We give the children practical, tangible support in developing control of their attention and their thinking. Therefore, we provide them with special materials – external mediators that will help young children hold in mind the structure of the story.

Choosing and showing substitute shapes helps the children to direct and maintain their own attention. Moving the shapes allows them to re-enact the most important events of the story. These external mediators help the children to focus on and remember important features and key events, rather than those that are simply salient. The madiators also help them to organise their attention and their mental activity.

The benefits of this programme

For younger children the biggest difficulty is holding the structure of the story in mind. A visual model is a plan for retelling a story. When a child knows the structure of a story he/she is empowered to become very active in retelling it. The aim is for the teacher to support the children in recreating teacher generated visual models at first and then, gradually, to enable them to create their own visual models and their own stories.

GOLDILOCKS AND THE THREE BEARS
INTRODUCTION TO THE STORY

AIMS

- To introduce the traditional story "Goldilocks and the Three Bears".
- To provide opportunities to listen to, understand and master the content of a traditional story.
- To evoke rich emotional understanding and the capacity to empathise.
- To share responses, feelings and personal experiences.
- To identify the elements of the story – characters and objects.
- To build familiarity with the distinctive patterns of the story.
- To develop knowledge of the main characters.
- To reinforce concepts about relative size – big, medium and small.
- To practise linking language to appropriate expressive movement.
- To hone understanding of intonation as a marker of expressive meaning.
- To establish recognition of characters through their distinctive intonation and movements.
- To foster understanding of the meaning of the story.

PROCEDURE

Once Upon a Time...

- Before telling the story, arrange an attractive special Storytelling Space (e.g. use cushions, a Storyteller's Garland, a Story Basket containing the book and some props, a bell).
- Discuss the book cover; ask the children to predict what the story is going to be about.
- Don't just read the text; tell the story as expressively as you can to provide a rich emotional experience; use the illustrations to help you explore and bring to life every episode. The more you put into the storytelling, the more the children will be able to take from it.
- Use props and visual aids (e.g. finger puppets, furniture) to maintain or refocus attention.

- Introduce traditional story language; e.g. "once upon a time."; "lived happily ever after".
- Develop active participation. Focus on rhythmic and

RESOURCES

For the teacher:

- ✓ Text of the story "Goldilocks and the Three Bears".
- ✓ Set of 8 A4 episode pictures.
- ✓ Storyteller's Garland, Bell and Chair.
- ✓ Story Basket with the story book, puppets and dolls.

LEARNING OUTCOMES

- Children can listen to the story and share their ideas about it.
- Children can name all the characters and describe them.
- Children can distinguish between big, medium and small characters and objects.
- Children can explain how the different characters feel at different points in the plot.
- Children can recognise different characters by the distinctive voices, intonations and movements associated with them.
- Children can imitate different characters and their emotional states through the appropriate use of distinctive voices, intonations and movements.

enjoyable repetitions. Encourage the children to join in with repeated refrains and any other parts of the story they already know.

Act Like a Bear

■ Talk about each of the characters. Help the children describe them in as much detail as possible. Describe the qualities that are visible or tangible (big, small, furry, strong, loud, soft, golden, brown, hot, cold ...) and those qualities that are invisible or intangible (curious, brave, foolish, hungry, sleepy, comfortable, shocked, sad, scared...).

■ Emphasise the characteristic colours and sizes of the characters; gold (yellow) for Goldilocks; brown for the bears; small for Baby Bear and Goldilocks, medium for Mummy Bear and big for Daddy Bear.

■ Choose individual children to demonstrate how the characters behave at different points in the story: how the bears walk (Daddy Bear – big steps, Mummy Bear – medium steps, Baby Bear – small steps); how Goldilocks tastes the porridge, tries the chairs, lies on the beds, sleeps and runs away.

■ Help the children to talk "just like the Three Bears" in big, medium and small voices (using contrasting voices and appropriate intonation helps the children build the ability to represent and understand the emotions and events the characters experience.)

■ Perform an action song based on the story with the children, if you know one, e.g. "When Goldilocks went to the House of Bears" by Robert Green.

Guess Who I Am?

■ Mime a character and ask the children to guess who it is.

■ Ask a child to mime a character and have the others guess.

■ To extend the game, ask the children to get into pairs; one of them mimes a character from the story while the other guesses who it is; then ask them to exchange roles.

Who Does This Belong To?

■ The story refers to various objects (bowls, spoons, chairs and beds) that come in different sizes; show the children a set of bowls which differ in size and discuss which bear uses which bowl; show them a chair or a bed and discuss who it belongs to and why; have them give Daddy Bear, Mummy Bear and Baby Bear the objects that belong to them etc.

GOLDILOCKS AND THE THREE BEARS
KINAESTHETIC MODELLING OF THE STORY – "SYMBOL THEATRE"

AIMS

- To support the development of deliberate memory – the ability to memorise a story structure.
- To promote focused attention – the ability to listen and attend to the whole of a story.
- To introduce the processes of substitution and kinaesthetic modelling.
- To establish the use of external mediators to help hold in mind the characters and events of a story.
- To practise identifying analogies between objects/characters and their substitute shapes.
- To improve comprehension using external mediators and kinaesthetic procedures ("Symbol Theatre").
- To foster the use of external mediators as tools for self-regulation.

RESOURCES

For the teacher:
✓ Text of the story "Goldilocks and The Three Bears".
✓ Storyteller's Garland, Bell and Chair.
✓ Large magnetic board.
✓ Magnetic substitute shapes: red circles; red squares, red rectangles, brown strips (big, medium and small); a yellow strip the same size as the smallest brown strip; a big grey rectangle.

For each child:
✓ Symbol Tray for substitute shapes approx. 60 cm x 45 cm.
✓ Set of substitute shapes matching the teacher's.

LEARNING OUTCOMES

- Children choose appropriate substitute shape for a story character or object.
- Children identify the characters and objects represented by substitute shapes correctly.
- Children move the correct substitute shapes as they appear in the telling of the story.
- Children move the substitute shapes appropriately to illustrate the actions of the characters.

PROCEDURE

Who Does This Belong To?

■ Place three strips (The Three Bears) in a row on the board. Make sure the children know that these strips are the Three Bears and can say which one is which.

■ The children take turns to choose objects for the Bears (e.g. give Baby his bowl, please).

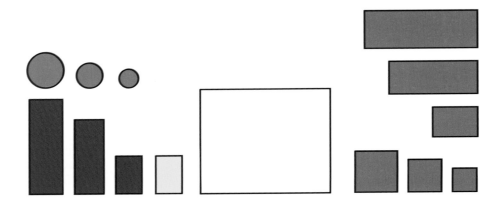

Kinaesthetic Modelling – "Symbol Theatre"

■ Give each child a Symbol Tray and a set of substitute shapes: red circles; red squares, red rectangles, brown strips (big, medium and small); a yellow strip the same size as the smallest brown strip; a big grey rectangle.

■ Ask them to arrange the Bears' bowls, beds and chairs inside their house, i.e. to arrange appropriate substitute shapes on the large grey rectangle in their trays (as shown below).

■ Now ask them to put the Bears and Goldilocks in the forest outside the house i.e. place the appropriate substitute shapes next to the grey rectangle in their trays (as shown below).

■ If necessary, model the procedure on the large magnetic board first and leave the layout on the board for the children to copy.

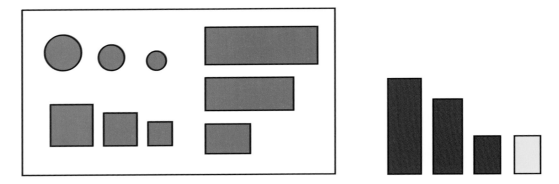

■ Tell the children they are going to "bring the story of Goldilocks to life"; you will tell the story; whenever you mention a character or an object they will hold up the right shape.

■ Tell the story, encouraging the children to hold up the relevant substitute shapes and use them to show what happens as the story unfolds. Suggest that they show Goldilocks trying each bowl of porridge, sitting on each chair, lying on each bed and falling asleep on the smallest.

■ To give an even more exciting and dangerous edge to Goldilocks' flouting of the rules, suggest that they overturn Baby Bear's bowl to show that Goldilocks eats all the porridge, and overturn Baby Bear's chair to show that she has broken it.

- SPEAK SLOWLY BECAUSE THE CHILDREN NEED TIME TO REACT TO EACH SCENE!!!

- Give the children a chance to choose the substitutes independently; encourage them to help each other choose the right substitutes, and to correct mistakes. If necessary prompt them by asking what shape, colour or size substitute they need for a specific character or object.

- Encourage the children to join in with repeated refrains and the parts of the story they already know.

- Tell the story again. This time encourage the children to move the substitute shapes in a way which illustrates the actions of the characters.

- If the children are likely to have a lot of difficulty, you could run this session several times, to help the children grasp the idea; model the correct behaviour by choosing the shapes yourself, musing aloud about your choices as you do so; gradually decrease the amount of support until the children are able to select the right substitutes independently.

RESOURCES

For teacher:

✓ Text of the story "Goldilocks and the Three Bears".

✓ Storyteller's Garland, Bell and Chair.

✓ Blank Story Skeleton.

✓ Large magnetic board.

✓ 8 (A4) episode pictures.

✓ 8 completed episode models (18 cm x 18 cm cards).

✓ Magnetic substitute shapes: red circles; red squares, red rectangles, brown strips (big, medium and small); a yellow strip the same size as the smallest brown strip; a big grey rectangle.

GOLDILOCKS AND THE THREE BEARS
VISUAL-SPATIAL MODELLING

AIMS

● To nurture analytical skills – use episode models to identify, summarise and sequence key narrative features.

● To practise matching episode pictures to episode models.

● To help children create and internalise an accurate "Story Skeleton" (an 8 episode story summary).

● To develop the ability to use the Story Skeleton as a prompt for retelling the story.

● To foster abstract thinking and early literacy skills – the ability to "read" (decode) episode models.

● To develop abstract thinking and early literacy skills – the ability to "write" (encode) episode models.

● To promote self-regulation.

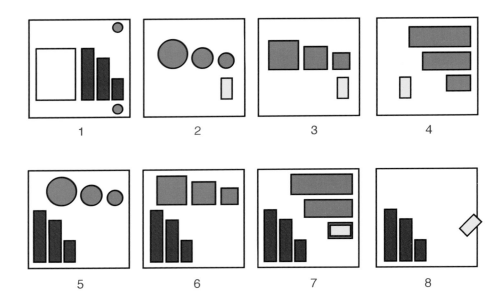

PROCEDURE

Match Episode Picture to Episode Model

■ On the magnetic board, make an Episode Model to match one of the Episode Pictures board. E.g. use three different sizes of circle (the bowls) and a yellow strip (Goldilocks) to represent the Episode Picture Goldilocks tastes the porridge.

■ Show the children 2 Episode Pictures, one that matches your model and one that doesn't; ask the children to choose the one that matches. If the children find this difficult, use questions to prompt them, e.g. "What can we see? That's right. There are three circles, and they are

different sizes. What sizes are they? Yes, a big one, a medium one and a small one. What could they be? Yes, Bears' bowls full of porridge, so we look for a picture with three bowls. What about this yellow strip? Of course, it's Goldilocks. So we need a picture with Goldilocks and the three bowls of porridge."

■ Continue until the children have seen all the episode models and matched them to the right pictures.

LEARNING OUTCOMES

· Children match individual episode models to episode pictures.

· Children sequence episode models to create a Story Skeleton.

· Children "read" episode models, i.e. use an arrangement of substitute shapes as a prompt for recounting the essential elements of an episode of the story.

· Children "write" episode models independently, i.e. use a visual-spatial arrangement of substitute shapes to represent the essential elements of an episode of the story.

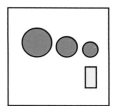   

Complete the Story Skeleton!

■ Put a blank Story Skeleton on the board or the table. Give out the eight episode models and ask the children to help you put them into the empty Story Skeleton in the right order, ensuring that there is at least one child responsible for each of the eight episodes.

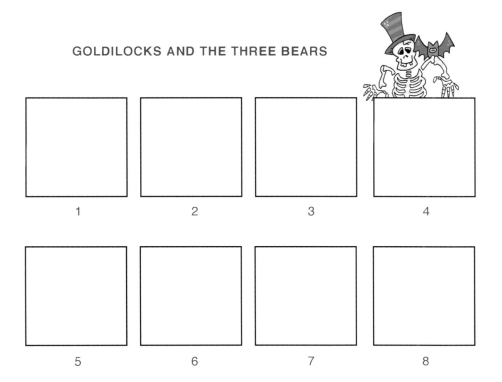

GOLDILOCKS AND THE THREE BEARS

1	2	3	4
5	6	7	8

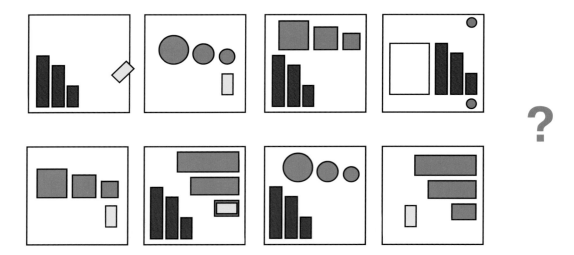

- Identify the two children with the beginning of the story; help them to put the first two episode models in the first two frames of the Story Skeleton, in the correct order.

- Next identify the four children with the middle of the story; finally the two children with the end of the story, e.g. "Who thinks that they have the models for the beginning of the story? The Three Bears go for a walk in the woods and Goldilocks tastes the porridge; 3 brown strips and a grey square, that's right the bears are walking in the forest; Goldilocks tries the porridge, 3 red bowls and a gold strip. Which goes first? OK, let's put them in these two frames, we have the beginning of the story. What happens next? Does Goldilocks try the beds.....no she tries the chairs first, so we look for? Three squares and a golden strip...who has that model?

- Encourage children without episode models to make suggestions and check for errors.

- End by summarising what has been achieved; the children have used all the episode models to make a Story Skeleton that will help them to remember the story.

DEVELOPMENTAL GAMES

PLAYING IN SMALL AND LARGE GROUPS CHILDREN DEVELOP PRODUCTIVE IMAGINATION, SYMBOLIC LITERACY, LANGUAGE AND COMMUNICATION SKILLS, FLEXIBLE THINKING, CREATIVE PROBLEM SOLVING, SELF-REGULATION AND SELF-ESTEEM

Overview

The Developmental Games programme helps children to develop the ability to imagine and to solve problems creatively, looking for their own novel solutions and learning to check that these solutions are plausible. They learn to look at a single simple feature and visualise an entire structure. They learn to consider how a given situation changes when we apply a set of rules to it. The programme emphasises language and communication skills, as well as helping children learn to concentrate, to recognise symbols, and to develop the social and emotional skills they require to work co-operatively in both small groups and in larger ones.

Why are these skills important?

Does creativity unfold spontaneously or can we foster its development? Are there steps we can take that go beyond celebrating evidence of self-expression when we come across it and taking care not to stifle the capacity for originality?

Creativity depends on the free flow of imagination and on flexible thinking. However, free flowing imagination and flexible thinking are most productive when we are able to direct them towards solving the tasks we set ourselves.

In addition to this, we need to develop a mindset that assumes that there can be many different solutions to problems and that urges us to seek actively for new ways of resolving them. Last, but not least, we need to have enough confidence in our ideas to express what we think; to be able to make good use of constructive feedback yet back our own ideas in the face of opposition; and to persevere when we discover that an idea hasn't worked as we expected.

How does this programme work?

The Developmental Games programme offers structured activities that encourage young children to develop and express feelings and ideas about the world in a variety of different contexts. These include looking at schematic drawings and visualising a range of possible pictures or stories; using geometric shapes to create a variety of different objects; visualising and creating their own completed pictures based on a schematic drawing or an incomplete image. In all these tasks a wide variety of responses are expected, with children encouraged to share their ideas, listen to others and offer feedback. A critical feature of the activities is the emphasis on encouraging children to explore a range of possible solutions to each task, either by carefully organising the materials they use or by specifically prompting them to offer several ideas.

There are also structured activities requiring practical problem solving and logical analysis. These include spotting errors in images; spotting discrepancies; matching pictures showing problems with pictures that show appropriate solutions; checking each other's work and offering feedback; temporal sequencing; and understanding a chain of events using if/then logic.

The benefits of this programme

As with all the Key to Learning programmes, Developmental Games deliberately and systematically focuses on the key cognitive processes of symbolisation, modelling, logical analysis and creative expression.

In particular, the programme emphasises language and communication skills, as well as helping children learn to concentrate, to recognise symbols and to develop the social and emotional skills they require to work co-operatively in small and larger groups.

IS IT A BIRD? IS IT A PLANE?

AIMS

- To name a variety of real objects suggested by a schematic line drawing.
- To find many possible solutions to the same problem.
- To develop imagination, creativity and originality.
- To develop perseverance and concentration.

 balloon, plate, ball, steering wheel, car wheel, etc.

 doll, soldier, man, etc.

 bath, boat, ship, bucket, bowl, etc.

 pyramid, tower, rocket, Christmas tree, sail, etc.

 snowman, doll, scarecrow, etc.

 dog, cat, duck, etc.

 train, car, carriage, etc.

RESOURCES

For the teacher:

✓ Several sheets of A4 paper, each with a different schematic line drawing ambiguous enough to suggest a variety of different toys.

LEARNING OUTCOMES

- Children hear a variety of answers to the question "What could this be?"
- Children give at least one independent answer to the question "What could this be?"

PROCEDURE

- Explain that an artist started to draw pictures of toys but did not have time to finish any of them. Can the children help to finish the pictures, by suggesting what the toy could be?
- Produce the schematic line drawings one at a time, and ask the children to suggest as many different toys as possible for each one.
- Young children typically give monosyllabic answers and copy each other's responses. Try asking for more detail, (e.g. size, colour) and for toys no one else has suggested.
- Many young children will find this game difficult; they find it hard to focus on a topic they have not chosen for themselves, and much easier to stay close to their own interests and concerns. For example, a drawing that reminds a child of a favoured toy may prompt extended talk about that toy, and a request to look at the next sheet. To develop perseverance and concentration you will need to engage with the child's concerns, but keep returning tactfully to the same outline until the children have suggested many different possibilities.

RESOURCES

For the teacher:

✓ Set of cards with a series of strips on them.

✓ Toy Robot.

For each child:

✓ Tambourine or any musical instrument.

LEARNING OUTCOMES

· Children follow a visual pattern to produce the correct sequence of sounds.

ROBOTS

AIMS

● To practise decoding visual messages.

● To develop symbolic thinking.

● To foster the ability to take turns and listen to others.

● To develop self regulation.

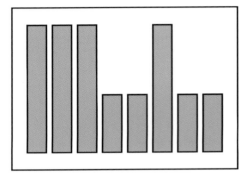 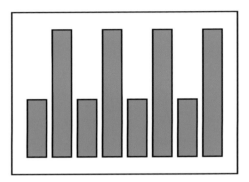

PROCEDURE

Robot Control

■ Sit in a semi-circle. Explain that we control Toy Robot by using different sounds. Clapping (or some other sounds e.g. tambourine, drum, etc.) activates Robot. Quick, loud sounds make Robot move quickly. Slow soft sounds make Robot walk on the spot. If the sound is very slow and quiet then Robot stands still.

■ Put Robot away, and then show a card with a long strip and a short one. Explain that the long strip means make a loud noise and the short one means make a soft noise.

■ Give each child a tambourine (or some other percussion instrument). Ask them to remind you what the long and the short strips represent, then to play the sounds shown on the card

■ Show another card with two long and two short strips. Discuss what the card shows (two loud notes and two soft ones); play the sounds and then collect the instruments.

Robot Moves Slowly, Robot Moves Fast

■ Get Robot out and give a child an instrument. Show a new card and ask the child to play the pattern s/he can see. The other children help by watching and listening to make sure that Robot gets the correct instructions.

■ When a child finishes a pattern correctly, move Robot as directed, then give the child a counter. If the pattern isn't correct ask another child to have a try. Continue until all the children have at least 2 counters. (You can vary the difficulty of the task by having cards with more/less complex patterns, as well as by giving the same card to several children).

FREEZE GAME

AIMS

- To develop self regulation.
- To promote understanding of symbols: know that a "clever picture". (schematic representation) can be used to convey a message.
- To practise decoding visual messages.

RESOURCES

For the teacher:
✓ 12 Freeze cards.

LEARNING OUTCOMES

- Children freeze in response to a visual message.
- Children freeze in the posture shown on a "clever picture" (schematic representation).
- Children create a "clever picture" to represent a posture.

PROCEDURE

Freeze Game

- Use either music or verbal instructions for this game.
- Ask the children to move around the room; when the music stops, the children must freeze. Alternatively, they must freeze when you say "1–2–3 freeze."
- Play several rounds where the children freeze in any posture they wish.
- Show a freeze card with a "clever picture" (schematic representation) of a posture. The children must freeze in the posture shown on the

card. They copy from their own perspective, i.e. if the figure holds up its left arm, the children hold up their right arms.

■ The child who freezes first chooses the next freeze card.

Opposite Freeze

■ Repeat the Freeze Game, but this time the children make an opposite posture to the one shown on the card. (Note that arms stretched out to the side/arms bent are opposites).

What's Wrong?

■ A child holds up the freeze card. The adult (or another child) copies, either correctly or incorrectly. If there has been a deliberate mistake, the child explains what's wrong.

Draw my Posture

■ Ask a child to create a posture and freeze in it; the other children draw a "clever picture" (schematic representation) of the posture on paper or small white boards.

■ Provide help by directing attention to the way the child has positioned his/her arms and legs.

ARTOGRAPHICS

CULTIVATES THE ESSENTIAL SKILLS REQUIRED BOTH FOR WRITING AND CREATIVE ARTISTIC EXPRESSION. DEVELOPS 'ART VISION' AND INTRODUCES DIFFERENT SYMBOLIC TOOLS: COMPOSITION, RHYTHM AND COLOUR

Overview

The Artographics programme helps young children to develop the skills they require both for writing and to express themselves creatively in art work. They have opportunities to develop the fine motor control and spatial awareness both tasks require. They learn that they can use marks on paper or manipulate plasticine, to create visual models of aspects of the world, using a variety of media to create expressive images. They learn how to represent subjects in movement as well as at rest, and how to use contrasting features of posture and facial expression to convey different emotions. They also learn to use colour to express emotion and create contrasting mood.

Why are these skills important?

Writing and imaginative expression in the visual arts are both highly complex activities involving similar sets of abilities. Writing is very difficult. Yet we expect children to be able to master it at a frighteningly early age despite its inherent difficulties, and often without adequate preparation. Writing involves the development of skills, for example, being able to grip the pencil correctly, and being able to control its movement and the pressure we exert on it. It involves the ability to remember, plan and execute a sequence of movements fluently. It also involves the ability to understand the purpose of the task — letters are not random shapes but symbols that allow us to record meaning.

Similarly we can identify some of the elements required to facilitate the creative production of representational images. First and foremost, children need to grasp the concept of a visual model — the idea that we can use marks on paper to represent what we see, and use these to communicate with others. Then they need opportunities to develop the skills required to manipulate pencil, charcoal, paint or plasticine; they need to practise organising and executing the sequence of movements required to actually produce the particular representation they have planned. They also need knowledge of techniques, for example, techniques for creating the impression of movement or for expressing emotion and mood.

How does this programme work?

The Artographics programme provides a progressive and structured framework for supporting the development of both writing and imaginative self-expression in art.

In the early stages there are tasks that introduce even very young children to the idea that marks on a page can be used to represent features of the visual environment; to develop spatial awareness by encouraging them to use all the available space on a page; and to introduce the symbolic use of warm and cold colours to represent happy or sad states. An important feature of the early part of the programme is the use of exercises to strengthen the fingers — Finger Gym®; the use of whiteboards and markers to develop confidence; and the use of Writing Rings to ensure that children grip their writing implement correctly.

In the later stages of the programme children observe phenomena before they draw, paint or model them in plasticine. They identify the visual elements that are critical for creating specific representations of, for example, an animal in movement or the expression on a face. There are tasks to extend understanding of the symbolic use of colour. Discussion and displays of work help to promote communication skills, self-confidence and pride in achievement.

The benefits of this programme

An important feature of this phase of the programme is the expectation that young children can and will learn by observing while an adult models complex, skilful behaviour. Opportunities to practise doing this are excellent preparation for the kind of learning experience children will meet (in much bigger classes) as they move on to school.

GRANDMOTHER AND NAUGHTY KITTEN

AIMS

- To develop pencil control.
- To develop spatial awareness when drawing/writing.
- To develop artistic rhythm.
- To fill all the available space with continuous curved lines when drawing.
- To master the psychographic skills of writing.
- To introduce substitution – the action of representing real objects and events by drawing.

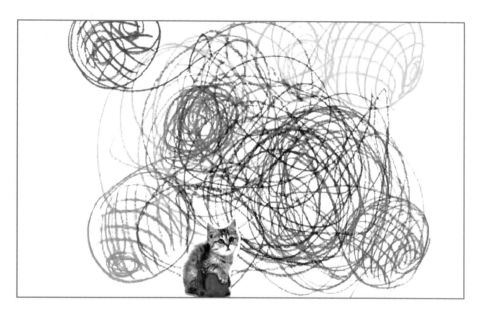

RESOURCES

For the teacher:
- ✓ Whiteboard and easel.
- ✓ Dry wipe markers.
- ✓ Ball of wool, Writing ring.
- ✓ Large sheet of paper.

For the children:
- ✓ Small white board (30cm x 20cm approx).
- ✓ Dry wipe marker.
- ✓ Board cleaners.
- ✓ Writing ring, Sheet of paper.

LEARNING OUTCOMES

- Children fill the available space with continuous curved lines.
- Children can explain that they have drawn Naughty Kitten's wool.

PROCEDURE

Naughty Kitten With a Ball of Wool

- Do Finger Gym® exercises in order to warm up the fingers using appropriate action songs.
- Tell the children the story of "Grandmother and the Naughty Kitten". Grandmother was knitting mittens for her grandchildren and she fell asleep. Naughty Kitten had been sitting next to her, and watching the wool. As soon as Grandmother fell asleep, Naughty Kitten pounced! She started playing with the ball of wool. She tugged and tugged at the ball of wool, just like this, and it began to unravel. She tugged some more and soon it wasn't a ball of wool any more, it was a tangle of lines.
- As you tell the story, unravel the wool. Let it fall onto a big white sheet of paper to show the wool unravelling to form smooth, random and tangled continuous lines. Put on a Writing Ring and show the children how to draw an image of the lines on the board. Model both correct grip and the rhythmic movement essential for the development of drawing/writing skills.

■ As you model the drawing skill, comment on your actions, e.g. "Look at the way I'm gripping the marker. My Writing Ring Finger rests on the marker like this, and my other fingers grip the marker like this. Look at the way I'm moving my hand; can you see how I'm creating the lines, they are long and smooth and all tangled up together; can you see how I'm using all the space to show the tangled wool? Now you have a go. Try to copy me."

■ Ask the children to imitate your work and draw the tangled wool on their boards. Give each child a Writing Ring before he or she starts to draw. Ask the children to put the ring on the finger that rests on top of the marker. Emphasise that only the Writing Ring Finger rests on the marker. Check that the children have put the rings on correctly before they begin to draw.

■ While the children are drawing, give them individual advice about how to use the drawing materials, encouraging them to fill the white board completely.

■ When you feel the children have had enough time to experiment on the boards, repeat the activity on paper using hand hugger pens that encourage the correct pencil grip. Allow the children to use different colours if you have them and they wish for them.

FALLING RAIN

AIMS

- To introduce substitution – the action of representing real objects and events by painting.
- To develop artistic rhythm.
- To fill all the available space with straight lines.

vertical rain

slanting rain

fine rain

heavy rain

RESOURCES

For the teacher:

✓ Small whiteboard and easel.

✓ Dry wipe markers.

For the children:

✓ Grey, white or pale blue paper.

✓ Brushes, Charcoal.

✓ Paint (preferably gouache).

LEARNING OUTCOMES

- Children can draw and/or paint straight lines.
- Children can explain that they have made a picture of rain.

PROCEDURE

- If possible, look carefully at falling rain before the session. Talk about the appearance of the rain, focussing on the appearance of the raindrops. Are they falling straight down (vertical rain), or are they falling at an angle (slanting rain)? Are the drops big (pouring) or small (spitting). Are there many big drops (heavy rain), or many small ones? (Fine rain).

- Remind the children of the different kinds of rain they have seen and show them how to draw different kinds of rain, using different lengths of straight lines "falling" vertically or horizontally, and filling all the available space. Comment on your actions as you do this.

- Give the children sheets of paper and ask them to draw or paint rain. If you have time repeat the activity using different media (charcoal/ paint, different coloured paper).

- While the children are drawing or painting, give them individual advice about how to use the materials, encouraging them to fill the whole sheet.

HAPPY AND SAD MUSIC

RESOURCES

For the teacher:

✓ A way of playing extracts from "The Four Seasons" by Vivaldi, or some other music with very distinct happy/sad moods.

For each child:

✓ A sheet of paper divided into two halves.

✓ Thick brushes.

✓ Red, yellow, blue and white paint (preferably gouache)

LEARNING OUTCOMES

• Children use warm colours to paint a happy feeling.

• Children use cold colours to paint a sad feeling.

• Children can name the feeling they have expressed through their choice of colour.

AIMS

● To produce abstract artistic compositions.

● To use colours as symbols for expressing mood.

PROCEDURE

Happy and Sad Music

■ Listen to some happy music and talk about how it makes us feel; listen to some sad music and talk about how it makes us feel. Talk about other things that make us feel happy and other things that make us feel sad.

■ Now connect these emotional states to appropriate colour symbolism. Talk about the colours which would be used to depict happy music; warm colours (red, orange yellow) from the top of the rainbow, the colours "nearest the sun." Talk about the colours which would be used to depict sad music – the cold colours from the blue part of the rainbow (blue, indigo violet).

■ Make an explicit connection between feeling warm and feeling happy; make an explicit connection between feeling cold and feeling sad. Happy music can make us feel warm and happy; sad music can make us feel cold and sad.

■ Give each child a piece of paper that has a fold or line down the middle. Ask the children to paint a sad feeling – the feeling we had when we listened to the sad music – on one half of the paper. Ask them to paint a happy feeling – the feeling we had when we listened to the happy music – on the other half.

■ Remind the children that we can use warm colours for happy feelings and cold colours for sad ones, but allow them to combine different colours in their own way.

■ End the session by asking each child to identify the sad and the happy halves of their picture.

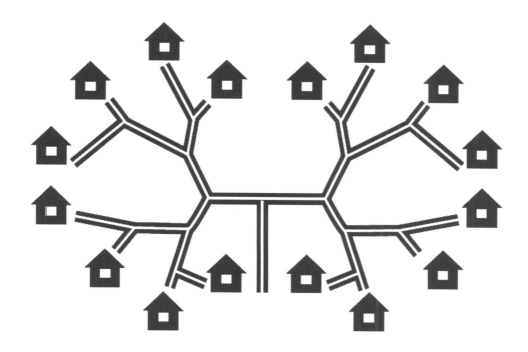

VISUAL-SPATIAL

**DEVELOPS SPATIAL AWARENESS AND THE ABILITY TO 'READ' MAPS.
CHILDREN LOOK AT OBJECTS IN SPACE AND USE SYMBOLS
TO REPRESENT WHAT THEY AND OTHERS SEE THROUGH
VISUAL MODELS – MAPS, SCHEMES AND PLANS**

Overview

This programme helps young children develop the ability to see the structure of objects and to visualise the connections between them. It is an introduction to understanding maps and visualising objects in space. Children use symbols to construct visual models (maps, schemes and plans) that represent what they see, to communicate their knowledge to others; and begin to use visual models to develop the crucial ability to think about what others can see.

Why are these skills important?

Many otherwise confident and competent adults left alone in an unfamiliar place with only a map to guide them to their destination, would find the task daunting if not impossible. Some people will find it difficult to make a plan of the ground floor of their own house let alone an unfamiliar house, a building with several floors or their immediate neighbourhood. Their visual-spatial abilities have remained underdeveloped.

When our ability to orientate in space is not adequately developed we find it difficult to "read" and construct maps, schemes and plans. But the consequences are far broader than this. Children who have problems with visualisation will have difficulties with Geography, Technical Drawing, Science and Mathematics.

On the other hand secure visual-spatial abilities help us to feel confident in our environment and facilitate practical problem solving. Moreover, as our visual-spatial awareness grows we learn to see what things look like from another's perspective and to understand that this may differ from what we see from our own. This has profound implications not just for cognitive but also for social and emotional development.

So the development of visual-spatial awareness is an important part of achieving our full human potential. Nevertheless, most Early Years programmes neglect it.

How does this programme work?

The Visual-Spatial programme focuses on helping children to orient themselves confidently in space; to acquire the vocabulary necessary for understanding and communicating relative spatial location (in front of/behind, to the left of/to the right of). They are offered opportunities to "read" and create plans of different spaces (part of a room, a whole room, a house, their school, their garden, their neighbourhood). To do this they use substitute shapes and later conventional symbols, assembled to form maps, schemes and plans. They learn about the function of such visual models as devices for recording precise information and conveying it to others. They learn to mark their position on such visual models. They learn to understand that what they see depends on where they are and on the direction of their gaze. They learn that the same applies to what others see too.

The benefits of this programme

Like all the other Key to Learning programmes the Visual-Spatial programme deliberately and systematically sets out to help children acquire key cognitive processes. Throughout this programme the emphasis is on opportunities to explore the use of substitute shapes as well as conventional signs and symbols to represent what we see. There are also opportunities to explore how we can assemble these substitute shapes, signs and symbols to record real spatial relationships in the form of plans and maps.

This focus makes the Visual-Spatial programme a particularly rich resource for developing symbolisation and visual modelling. Teachers may also find that the Visual-Spatial programme is a particularly valuable resource because it supports an essential but neglected aspect of cognitive development.

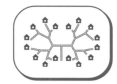

CAN WE HELP TEDDY?

AIMS

- To explore spatial concepts.
- To show that we can use symbols (substitute shapes) to represent real objects.
- To arrange substitute shapes on a piece of paper to represent a simple room layout.

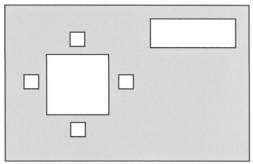

PROCEDURE

- Arrange some furniture in a room in a doll's house as shown in the plan above.
- Set the scene. Show Amanda to the children. Tell them that Amanda is having a birthday party. Everyone is having a wonderful time. Then she spots Teddy in a corner and he is crying! She asks why he is upset, tells him not to cry and offers to help. Teddy explains that Amanda has such a lovely room that he wants to arrange his furniture at home exactly the same way. However, he lives so far away that by the time he gets home he will have forgotten how to do it.
- Ask the children for their ideas about how to help Teddy remember the furniture arrangement. Thank children for any contributions. Help them reach the conclusion that Teddy needs a plan.
- Show the children the substitute paper shapes. Help them decide which shape can best represent the different pieces of furniture.
- Make sure the children are all facing the same direction.
- If necessary, model the procedure; show the children how to arrange the substitute shapes on a piece of card to represent the layout of Amanda's room.
- Give each child a set of shapes and ask them to arrange the shapes on card to represent the layout of the furniture.
- Check the children's work, and discuss any problems before asking them to stick down the shapes.

RESOURCES

For the teacher:

- ✓ Dolls' house and furniture for one room (table, 4 chairs, bed).
- ✓ Substitute shapes: square for the table, 4 squares for chairs and rectangle for the bed.
- ✓ Doll Amanda.
- ✓ Teddy Bear.

For the children:

- ✓ Substitute shapes: (square table, 4 square chairs, rectangular bed).
- ✓ Sheet of coloured paper.
- ✓ Glue stick.

LEARNING OUTCOMES

- Children can arrange substitute shapes accurately to represent the layout of furniture in a room.

HIDE THE BEETLE

AIMS

- To develop spatial awareness.
- To practise drawing plans.
- To mark items on a plan within a perimeter.

RESOURCES

For the teacher:

✓ Doll's room with furniture: circular table, rectangular

✓ Bookcase, square chair and triangular stool.

✓ Whiteboard.

✓ Dry marker.

✓ Small plastic beetle.

For the children:

✓ Sheets of paper.

✓ Pencils.

LEARNING OUTCOMES

- Children can draw a perimeter of a doll's room, placing the walls, doors and windows correctly.

- Children can draw substitute shapes on the plan to represent the layout of items of furniture.

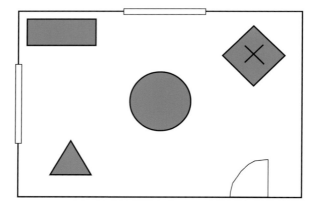

PROCEDURE

Guided Work

■ Make sure all the children are facing in the same direction before you begin the activity.

■ Place a doll's room with some furniture in front of the children. Place a whiteboard so that it is level with the doll's room.

■ Tell the children that everyone is going to make a plan of the doll's room.

■ Explain that we start with walls, doors and windows first and put the furniture in later, because it will make drawing the plans much easier.

■ Take the furniture out of the doll's room.

- Draw the perimeter of the room on the whiteboard. Show the children how to mark walls, doors and windows on the plan. Take care to make your drawing the same size as the sheets of drawing paper the children will be using.
- Give out the drawing paper.
- Ask the children to draw the perimeter of the room, marking the walls, windows and doors.

Review

- Collect the children's plans. Compare the children's plans to the plan you have drawn on the whiteboard and to the actual doll's house. Always point at the feature you are comparing – e.g. point at the wall in the doll's house, the same wall on the whiteboard and the same wall on the child's drawing.
- Focus on correlating the positions of the windows and doors in the doll's room, and on the plans of the doll's room. Refer to your plan, children's plans and the doll's room E.g. look, on my plan the windows are on the same side as in the doll's room. Jack has done the same on his plan. Ben's plan is different. Where is Ben's window? Is it on the same side as the window in the doll's room? Where is Jack's door? Is it on the same side as the door in the doll's room? Is it on the same side as the door on my plan? Etc.
- Focus on correlating the lengths of the walls in the doll's room, and on the plans of the doll's room. Refer to your plan, the children's plans and the doll's room. E.g. which wall of the doll's room is the longest? And which wall on the plan here on the whiteboard? And which wall here in Marina's plan is the longest? Does the length of the wall in Sara's plan match the length of the wall in the doll's house? Etc.

Consolidate and Extend

- Make sure the children are all facing in the same direction before you begin the activity.
- Return plans of the doll's room that have been drawn correctly to the children who drew them.
- Give new pieces of paper to any children who made significant errors in drawing their room outline (e.g. short walls where there should be long ones, or a mirror image of the room.)
- Arrange the four pieces of furniture in the doll's room.
- Review the substitute shapes required to represent the items of furniture and draw them on the whiteboard; make sure that the substitute shapes you draw on the whiteboard are approximately the size you expect to see on the children's plans.
- Ask those children whose perimeter drawings are correct to add the furniture to their plan (i.e. by drawing substitute shapes to represent the layout); help anyone who needs to correct an outline to do this before they add the furniture.

Review

- Collect the children's plans. Compare their plans to the plan you have drawn on the whiteboard and to the actual doll's house. Always point at the feature you are comparing – e.g. point at the wall in the doll's house, the same wall on the whiteboard and the same wall on the child's drawing.
- Focus on the position of the furniture within the doll's room (e.g. in the doll's room the table is in the middle, and it's in the middle of the room in my plan on the whiteboard too. The sofa is by this short wall, and it's by this short wall here on the whiteboard. David drew his table exactly where it is in the room, here in the middle, and he drew the sofa by the short wall, exactly where it is in the room.
- This session is demanding – you may find that you wish to repeat it, introducing new pieces of furniture.

Extend

- Play Hide the Beetle.
- Ask one of the children to hide a toy beetle under a piece of furniture in the doll's room.

- Ask the other children not to peep whilst the child hides the beetle.
- Ask the child to put a cross on his or her plan to show where the beetle is hiding.
- Ask another child to find the beetle, using the plan. The seeker may not just move the furniture. S/he needs to point to the position of the beetle or say where it is hiding, looking only to check that s/he is right.
- When a seeker finds the beetle, it is his or her turn to hide the beetle.
- Repeat the game until everyone has had a turn.

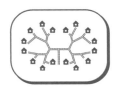

FROM A DIFFERENT POINT OF VIEW

AIMS

- To know that an object can look different if you look at it from different sides.
- To learn that viewpoint or perspective (what we see) depends on orientation in space (position).
- To make plans involving a relatively complex arrangement of tables and chairs.
- To decide which shape is most appropriate for each part of a plan.
- To identify personal position in a room and mark it on a plan.

RESOURCES

For the child:
- ✓ Selection of substitute shapes, Giraffe – soft toy.
- ✓ Glue stick, Sheet of coloured paper or card.

LEARNING OUTCOMES

- Children notice that they can see a different aspect of a giraffe when they look at it from a different perspective.
- Children can mark their own position on a plan of tables and chairs.

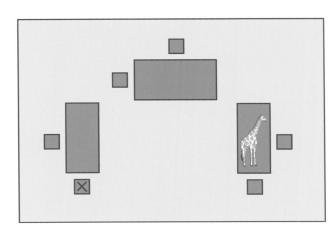

PROCEDURE

- Create a seating plan similar to the one in the diagram; put Giraffe on a table.
- Ask children to say which bit of the giraffe they can see. For example, a child on seat A might say that s/he can see Giraffe's tail; one on seat B, Giraffe's ear; one on seat C Giraffe's face.
- Children on seats B and D can both see Giraffe's ear; take the opportunity to point out that they can see different ears, and to introduce the terms right ear and left ear.
- Move the giraffe to a different table and ask the children what they can see now.
- Keep Giraffe on the same table but change its orientation; ask what the children see.
- Discuss the layout of the tables and chairs; focus on the fact that things look different depending on where you are sitting. For example, seat A faces a table and has a table to its right, while D has tables to the right and the left, but not directly in front.
- You could swap seats and repeat the discussion, focussing on what looks different.

- Tell the children they are going to make a plan of the room showing their tables and chairs.

- Give each child a sheet of coloured paper; help them draw the perimeter, showing windows, walls and doors

- Decide which substitute shapes to use for tables and chairs. Give each child a set of shapes (you may wish to give out only enough shapes for one table and its chairs at a time).

- Ask the children to look at the layout of the tables and chairs.

- Help the children arrange the shapes, one table and its chairs at a time; when the plan is correct stick down the shapes; have each child mark the place where s/he sits with an X.

CREATIVE MODELLING

THROUGH SHARED ACTIVITY CHILDREN DISCOVER SYMMETRY
AND PATTERN BY MANIPULATING GEOMETRIC SHAPES TO CREATE
ARTISTIC COMPOSITIONS OF THE WORLD AROUND THEM.
DEVELOPS CO-OPERATIVE AND SOCIAL SKILLS

Overview

Creative Modelling develops creativity and allows children to work together to realise different ideas and to create artistic compositions by exploring materials, colours and textures.

Through Creative Modelling we are able to help children learn how to create representations of aspects of the real world; and in this process we help them to develop mental models of, and emotional responses to, the realities they learn to represent.

Why are these skills important?

The materials developed for the programme pare down the process of creating representational images to the most essential building blocks. Consequently it is very easy for young children – and their less artistically inclined teachers! – to satisfy the desire to create credible representational images long before they have developed the fine motor control needed for the skilled manipulation of the tools of the artist's trade. With the most difficult technical elements of the task well supported, young children are able to concentrate on mastering those elements of the task that are within their grasp. These elements include such basics as identifying shapes and colours, using lines and dots, using all the space available and grasping symmetry and pattern. Crucially, they also include developing a personal response to the subject of the composition.

Through shared activity children learn to share ideas through talk. They learn to control their own behaviour and attention. They learn how to work together and how to help each other maintain focus.

How does this programme work?

These sessions are built on the use of geometric shapes, cut out of felt, in a variety of sizes and colours. What is more the felt feels nice to the touch. Placing the pieces provides a soothing tactile pleasure that encourages persistence and participation.

Working with a teacher, young children are enabled to create compositions across some of the most important genres of representational art, urban and rural landscapes, still life, representations of functional and decorative objects and of animals.

The benefits of this programme

Creative Modelling does more than allow children to represent their environment and express a personal response to it. It also:

- Provides children with a chance to develop the social skills required for group work.
- Allows children to learn from each other.
- Helps children analyse and understand their environment, teaching a number of cognitive skills. These include learning how to identify features of geometric shapes (colour and size); how to use the shapes symbolically, as substitutes for real objects or parts of real objects in representational images; and how to choose and organise substitutes to create representations (visual models) of ever more complex objects.
- Helps children extend their knowledge and understanding of the world as they use talk, role-play, song, dance and the creation of representations to explore the various themes that run through the programme.

It is relatively simple to prepare the session backgrounds using the descriptions and illustrations provided in the notes for the sessions. Because the material is so easy to use – and because the tasks the children are asked to complete are so finely graded and achievable – the programme supports very young artists in creating work that would otherwise remain beyond their capabilities.

BIG BEAR, LITTLE BEAR

AIMS

- To develop curiosity and creativity.
- To create a representation of bears in a winter landscape.
- To use a given procedure to construct the structures of big and little bears.
- To work in a group.
- To develop a model of a wild animal.

PROCESSES

Recognise the common feature of matching circles (size). Do this by comparing pairs of circles. Place the circles on top of each other or hold them up, one against the other.

Distinguish between circles of different sizes.

Substitute brown circles for parts of a bear's body.

Construct a model of a bear (i.e. a physical representation that can be remembered, visualised and referred to as a map of the bear's structure).

Develop artistic symbolisation – use colour and rhythm to create the shapes of a big and a little bear; express a personal response towards the topic.

Develop understanding of transformation – demonstrate relationships between opposites.

PROCEDURE

- Look at a Bear and talk about it; name the main parts of the bear's visible body structure – the head, the body, the ears and the paws. Talk about the bear's appearance, and show the children the rocking movement.

- On a prepared background show the children how to construct a representation of a big brown bear using brown circles for the body parts and small white, red and black circles to create the facial features. Talk to the children about what you are doing as you demonstrate each step of the procedure. Repeat the procedure to make a Small Bear using the set of smaller circles.

RESOURCES

The Wood in Winter:

✓ Several blue or grey backgrounds with evergreen and/or bare deciduous trees in a snowy landscape; bear.

Handout material:

✓ Brown white, black and red circles. For the Big Bear you will need a big brown circle for the body, a medium sized one for the head and four small ones for the paws and the ears. You will also need some white, black, and red circles for creating mouth, nose and eyes. You will need the same set of circles in smaller sizes for the Small Bear.

LEARNING OUTCOMES

Common to all sessions:

- Children listen to the teacher and engage with the group task.
- Children follow simple rules of social behaviour.
- Children cooperate with peers and adults.
- Children participate enthusiastically and actively for the whole session.   →

- Children switch quickly from one activity to another (e.g. from modelling to listening to a story).
- Children use the construction material functionally i.e. they know what the brown circles represent, and where and how to use them.
- Children treat the construction material with due care.
- Children correct their errors when prompted.
- Children take part in group discussion, and volunteer answers to the teacher's questions.
- Children take pride in their work.

Specific outcomes:

- Children use size to distinguish between circles.
- Children work independently, following the given procedure to construct big and small bears correctly.

- Help the children to make their own brown bears. Give them prepared backgrounds and ask them to add a big and a small bear. First give out sets of brown circles for the big bears.
- Use questions to prompt the children if they run into difficulty making the shape correctly e.g. which part of the bear are you going to do next? Is the head bigger than the body? Etc.
- Now ask the children to repeat the process to make a little brown bear.
- When they have made the bears, encourage the children to admire them.
- You may wish to end the session by reading aloud a children's story involving bears e.g. "Brown Bear in a Brown Chair" by Irina Hale, "Big Bear Little Bear" by Martin Waddell or any of the teddy bear stories by Susanna Gretz.

SWITCH ON THE LIGHTS

AIMS

- To develop curiosity and creativity.
- To complete and transform a representation of buildings at night.
- To use a given procedure to transform a feature (switch on the lights).
- To work in a group.
- To know about electric lights.

RESOURCES

Our Street:

✓ A black background with the moon in the sky and flats with dark windows.

Handout material:

✓ Yellow squares for light shining through the windows.

LEARNING OUTCOMES

All the common programme outcomes and in addition these session-specific ones:

- Children use a procedure to transform all the dark windows into lighted windows.
- Children take part in group discussion, volunteer answers to the teacher's questions.
- Children admire the beauty of their street with light shining through all the windows.

PROCESSES

Recognise the common feature of matching squares (colour). Do this by comparing pairs of squares. Hold them up against each other side by side.

Substitute yellow squares for electric light shining through a window.

Distinguish between dark and yellow squares.

Construct a model of houses with lights shining through the windows at night (i.e. a physical representation that can be remembered, visualised and referred to as an aid in organising thought).

Develop artistic symbolisation – use colour and rhythm to create an expressive image of a complex human activity. Respond personally to the topic.

Develop understanding of transformation – demonstrate relationships between opposites.

PROCEDURE

- Talk about "Our Street". People live in the flats; the flats have windows, just like the ones in our classroom; they are made of glass; during the day light comes in through the windows; in the evening it starts to get dark and we switch on the lights on so we can see.

- Show the children how to "switch on a light" (cover a dark window with a yellow square).

- Ask the children to help you "switch all the lights on" (i.e. cover all the dark windows with yellow squares). Allow the children to work independently. Prompt them if they need help (e.g. you have switched on so many lights, the street looks amazing. But it's very dark over here. Can we put some lights on?). Encourage the children to take pride in their work.

CHICKS AMONG THE DANDELIONS

RESOURCES

The Meadow:

✓ A green background with dandelion stalks, one or two dandelions, a sun with sunbeams radiating out, a hen and a chick.

Handout material:

✓ Circles in a variety of sizes and colours (including white and several shades of yellow); a variety of geometric substitutes for making stalks, leaves and features of chicks, e.g. green strips, small red triangles, orange triangles, orange semi-circles, small black circles.

AIMS

● To develop curiosity and creativity.

● To complete and transform a detailed landscape.

● To use a given procedure to add and modify specified features.

● To follow a set of instructions.

● To work with the teacher and other children as part of a group.

● To develop awareness of seasonal change.

PROCESSES

Construct a model of a meadow in summer with dandelions and chicks, i.e. a physical representation that can be remembered, visualised, and referred to as an aid in organising though. This includes constructing a model of the physical structure of a chick's body.

Compare and categorise geometric objects. Distinguish between them by colour, shape or size. Do this by visually comparing pairs of objects. Place the objects on top of each other or hold them up against each other.

Substitute geometric shapes (symbols) for objects; relate a spatial arrangement composed of symbols to a real natural object.

Practise perceptive modelling. Analyse an object visually. Visualise which parts can be represented by different substitutes. Construct a model of the object using an appropriate spatial arrangement of the substitutes. Relate the model to reality.

Modify and transform images. Vary their features.

Develop artistic symbolisation – learn to use colour, size, rhythm and symmetry to produce an expressive image, and learn to express a personal response towards the subject.

Develop understanding of transformation – grasp opposites and temporal sequences.

PROCEDURE

- If possible, take the children out to look for some dandelions before the session; find some with a flower head and some with fluffy seed heads if you can. Compare the yellow flower heads, the leaves and the white fluffy seed heads.

- Play "dandelion clocks"; blow the seeds off a dandelion. Count the number of puffs required to blow all the seeds away – that's the time on the dandelion clock.

- Look at "The meadow". Focus on the dandelions, and talk about them ("They have green leaves, long stalks and soft yellow flowers").

- Name the flower; if the group went out to find dandelions talk about the experience.

- Ask the children to "plant more dandelions all over the meadow."

- Prompt them if necessary (short green strips for leaves, a longer one for the stalk, yellow circles for flower heads), When the meadow is full of yellow dandelions, admire the work.

- Focus on the hen. Sing an appropriate song or recite a poem about chickens. Talk about what hens and chicks eat ("They scratch in the ground to peck up seeds, worms, etc.").

- Tell the children that the mother hen in the picture feels very sad. Ask them if they can guess why she feels sad (she has only one chick with her, the rest are all hiding), Ask the children how they could help her (put the rest of her chicks in the meadow).

- Ask the children to put some more chicks in the meadow. Do not demonstrate the procedure or tell the children what steps to take to construct the chicks unless they run into difficulties.

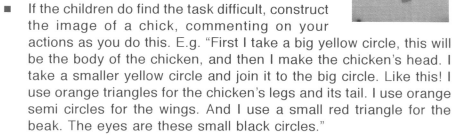

- If the children do find the task difficult, construct the image of a chick, commenting on your actions as you do this. E.g. "First I take a big yellow circle, this will be the body of the chicken, and then I make the chicken's head. I take a smaller yellow circle and join it to the big circle. Like this! I use orange triangles for the chicken's legs and its tail. I use orange semi circles for the wings. And I use a small red triangle for the beak. The eyes are these small black circles."

- Use questions and prompts to encourage the children to make their chicks look as if they are moving about. E.g., "Is your chick looking for food in the grass? Is your chicken looking at the clouds? Is your chick running over to its mum? Is this chick talking to his sister?" etc.

LEARNING OUTCOMES

All the common programme outcomes and in addition these session-specific ones:

- Children understand and transform a model of a meadow with adult support.

- Children analyse the structure of a chick; they use geometric shapes to reconstruct it independently.

- Children discuss their work, using rich, expressive vocabulary to describe the natural world as well as their own thoughts and emotions.

- Children show their enjoyment of the session (e.g. by staying on task; admiring their completed work; talking about the beauty of their work and the beauty of those aspects of the real world their work reflects).

- If necessary, show the children how to alter the appearance of a chick by careful placement of beak, wings, feet, eyes...

- When the children have finished, look at the chicks, and talk about them (they are smaller than the hen, they are doing lots of different things, pecking for food, looking at the sky, running about, etc).

- While the children are constructing their chicks replace some of the yellow dandelion "flowers" with "fluffy white seed heads."

- Tell the children that while they were making the chicks, something happened to some of the dandelion flowers. Ask the children if they can spot what has happened (some dandelions have turned white); ask if they can say why (the flowers have transformed into seeds). Ask the children to "transform all the dandelion flowers" by replacing yellow circles with white ones.

- To end the session, the children admire the beauty of the meadow; and sing an appropriate song or recite an appropriate poem about chicks.

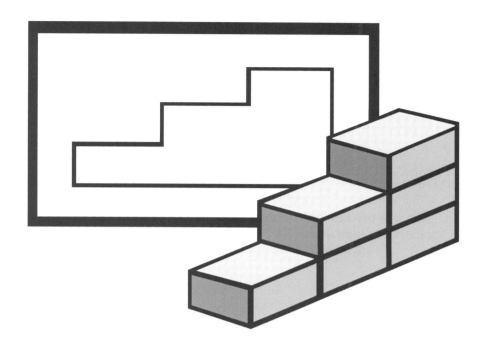

CONSTRUCTION

**DEVELOPS MATHEMATICAL AND GOAL DIRECTED BEHAVIOUR.
CHILDREN ANALYSE THE STRUCTURE OF OBJECTS, PLAN,
EXPLAIN THEIR PLANS AND EXECUTE THEM USING
WOODEN MODULAR BUILDING BLOCKS**

Overview

The Construction programme develops children's ability to plan; to articulate what they have planned; to analyse the structure of objects (e.g. buildings, bridges, fences, etc); and to analyse the relationships between their different parts. To do this they learn to use an important mental tool. This is a scheme (a drawn plan or a structure) which acts as a visual model of a structure that the children will build for themselves using a set of modular building blocks. Through the use of a range of schemes in a variety of tasks, children learn to look at objects from different perspectives and to think carefully about what they need to do to build a given structure before they start building.

Why are these skills important?

One of the most important characteristics of successful adults is that they see themselves as architects of their own lives; they do not act on impulse alone, but are able to set themselves goals, make plans that will allow them to achieve those goals, and then execute those plans. The Construction programme aims to foster goal directed behaviour, and to help children to master their impulsivity.

How does this programme work?

The Construction programme offers structured activities which help young children to use building blocks to develop key cognitive abilities. There are tasks which involve using symbolic representation, for example, substituting 2D shapes on a drawing for 3D blocks, and then using the arrangement of such shapes as the visual model – the plan – for constructing a specific structure. There are tasks which demand a combination of logical analysis and symbolisation. For example, the children may analyse a plan to work out which blocks they will need and how they will need to place them to create the 3D structure represented; or they may create their own visual models to represent 3D structures that others can build.

Further tasks develop logical analysis and creative production. For example, the children devise their own solutions to overcome such problems as building a road wide enough for two vehicles, or a bridge tall enough to allow a big boat to pass beneath it. To do this they must understand the relationship between the design of the structure they are to create and its function; plan and build a design that actually works; set criteria for judging that the completed design does, in fact, work; and then check their own and others' work against these criteria.

The benefits of this programme

A key feature is the opportunity to develop mathematical concepts and language because the programme demands the use of a rich mathematical vocabulary in a practical, visual context. As they talk about their work the children have the opportunity to access vocabulary that includes the names of the building blocks and the 2-D shapes to which they correspond in plans; names for concepts such as edge, side, corner, face, flat, solid, straight, curved, plan, elevation; for actions such as balance, build, connect, put together, take apart, stack; and for prepositions and prepositional phrases such as on top of, to the left of, to the right of, next to, under, etc. The children also acquire a practical understanding of the physical properties of the shapes – not least a practical understanding of their relative sizes which should facilitate their understanding of measurement.

The work that the children are able to accomplish during structured sessions can be enhanced if they are provided with information and stories relating to the types of structures they are being asked to create, for example, you could take them out to look at a bridge or a building site. They will also benefit from access to the building materials during free flow play and encouragement to plan and give shape to their own visions.

DRIVE OVER, FLOAT UNDER
CONSTRUCTING A ROAD BRIDGE TO MEET GIVEN CRITERIA

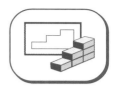

AIMS

- To develop the ability to build a structure to meet given criteria.
- To foster analytical thinking.
- To elicit the ability to analyse a construction before building it: identify the purpose of the structure, identify the main functional components, identify necessary physical characteristics, e.g. width, height, steps for a footbridge, and ramps for a road bridge.
- To practise constructing spans and piers.
- To develop the ability to identify and name the most important functional components of a structure.
- To review the idea that the specific function of a structure governs our choice of blocks.
- To foster understanding of spatial orientation and symmetry.
- To practise using the language of spatial orientation, e.g. over, under, next to, across, on both sides, opposite, beyond, etc.
- To encourage children to work together as a team.

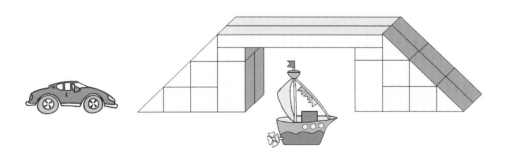

PROCEDURE

Structure of a Bridge (Analysis and Explanation)

- Show the children a picture of a bridge over the river. Help the children to describe its main parts (ramps, piers and span), length (long or short) and width (wide or narrow). Ask, "What does the ramp look like? (A slope); Why wasn't the ramp built with steps? (It is for cars).

Transport Bridge (Building by Imitation – Copycat Step by Step)

- Now build a transport bridge step-by-step. Explain what building blocks you use for each functional part of the bridge. Draw their attention to how symmetrically the piers are placed exactly opposite each other and how precisely the beam rests on the top of them.

RESOURCES

For the teacher:

- ✓ Pictures of road and rail bridges.
- ✓ 4 cuboids, 2 bricks, 2 short boards, 8 prisms.

For each child:

- ✓ 6 prisms, 8 cubes, 2 cuboids, 1 long board.
- ✓ Strip of blue paper 14 cm wide (river).
- ✓ Car 4 cm wide and boat 7 cm high.
- ✓ Access to all the blocks (final activity only).
- ✓ Collection of small cars, boats and play people.

LEARNING OUTCOMES

- Children can explain differences between a road bridge and a footbridge.
- Children can build copies of the road bridge from the model.
- Children can build road bridges to meet given criteria.
- Children can use a range of vocabulary relating to spatial orientation.
- Children can build stable structures, skilfully and precisely.
- Children can check that structures meet given criteria.
- Children work together co-operatively.

- During the explanation use as much spatial vocabulary as possible, e.g. on the top, next to, opposite to, under, over, on both sides. Check that the children understand.
- Give the children a set of blocks and cars and ask them to build a road bridge.

High Enough – Wide Enough (Building According to Given Criteria)

- Give the children a set of bricks, cars 4 cm wide, boats 7 cm high, a blue paper strip 14 cm wide and ask them to build a bridge over a wide river. This time do not show a real example (3D model or diagram), but describe the criteria: the bridge needs to go over a wide river; cars should be able to go over it and boats to sail under.
- Children need to meet the given criteria, e.g. build the bridge wide enough to allow cars to travel over it, high enough to allow boats to pass beneath it and the pillars strong enough to support such a structure. They add ramps for the cars to drive up to and down from the span.
- After they have completed their project take one of the cars and say you will test the bridges before they are opened to the public. Drive the car over all the bridges in turn commenting at each one about its width, strength, how well the blocks are joined together and how symmetrical the structure is. Now test the height of the bridge by "sailing" a boat under it and commenting about how it spans the whole width of the river. If the bridge passes the test, give the child a Builder's Certificate.
- Let the children use their small toys for imaginative play once their structures have been completed.

Shared Construction Activity: Road Bridge and Foot Bridge (Meet the Criteria)

- Ask the children to build a combined road bridge and footbridge over a wide river. Do not provide any physical model. Instead, describe the following criteria. The bridge spans a wide river. It is high enough to allow boats to pass under it. Cars and pedestrians can both use the bridge safely at the same time. Cars drive on ramps to get onto the bridge and off it again. One  of the ramps leading to the span is short and steep; the other ramp is long and slopes gently. There are steps for the pedestrians, and barriers to separate them from road traffic.
- Divide the children into groups of two or three; each group builds a version of their bridge and tests it using play people and small vehicles.

Tidy Up Time

- At the end of the session, encourage the children to dismantle their structures and to sort all the building blocks into the correct trays, i.e. trays with picture cards corresponding to the shapes of the different blocks.
- To help make tidying up more enjoyable, make a game of it. For example, the teacher might close the session by explaining to the children that animals like to play with building blocks too. Each of them has their favourite: Frog likes cubes, Giraffe likes bricks, Bear likes cuboids, Hedgehog likes triangular prisms and Elephant likes long boards... The teacher could put an animal in the correct tray, and then show the children how to give each animal its favourite blocks, demonstrating how to put the blocks away in the correct trays.
- Ask the children to give each animal their favourite building blocks.

- Play an appropriate piece of music, e.g. "Can We Fix It? – Bob the Builder", which the children will come to associate with clearing away. Use a timer to see how quickly the clearing away can be completed!

BLOCKS' BEDTIME
WHERE IS MY BED?
MATCHING BLOCKS TO THEIR PLANS

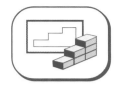

AIMS

- To develop the ability to analyse building blocks by shape and size (width, height, length).
- To familiarise children with all the possible orientations of building blocks.
- To introduce a kinaesthetic procedure for matching building blocks to their outlines.
- To practise placing blocks on drawn outlines so that they match exactly.
- To practise differentiating between building blocks on the basis of their spatial qualities.
- To practise recognising building blocks from a set of graphic representations on a three-view scheme.
- To help children relate the front, top and side-views of a building block.
- To practise creating accurate three-view schemes of building blocks independently.

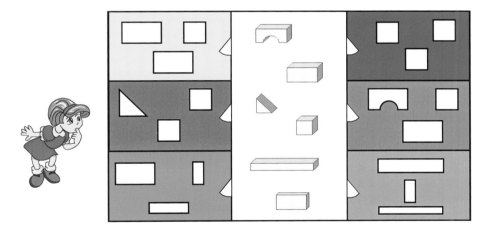

RESOURCES

For the teacher:

- ✓ Blocks' Bedrooms – Full size coloured plans of blocks: the plans should show three views (front, top, side) of the blocks and should gradually increase in complexity.
- ✓ Blocks' Bedroom coloured plan (full size) with six bedrooms.

For each child:

- ✓ Full size plans showing three views of blocks (cube, brick, cuboid, small prism, arch, short board).
- ✓ Building Blocks for matching to the plans (3 per plan).

LEARNING OUTCOMES

- Children place blocks on drawn outline plans so that they match exactly.
- Children put blocks to sleep in the correct bedrooms.
- Children put blocks to sleep in the correct beds.
- Children turn blocks, if necessary, to match them to the right beds. →

PROCEDURE

Blocks' Bedtime – Where is my Bed?

- Start by saying, "We already know that the building blocks family is very big one. They all live together in a big house. All the blocks need their own special beds to help them sleep comfortably. Let us look at the Cubes' Bedroom."
- Put a plan of the Cubes' Bedroom on the table. Take three cubes and show the children how to put them on top of the plan so that they match exactly. To make sure the children understand what you mean by "match exactly", place one of the blocks incorrectly and wait to see if anyone spots the mistake. Draw attention to it if necessary. If children find the concept of "matching exactly" difficult, try showing them how you can make outlines of blocks by drawing around a block on a piece of paper.

- Children identify and name blocks by feel.
- Children match blocks correctly to three-view schemes.
- Children identify the top, front and side-views of structures they have built.
- Children can name the blocks they can see from three different views of a structure.

■ Show the children the Block People one by one: Cube, Brick, Cuboid, Prism Cylinder... (It is up to the teacher to decide how many building blocks to introduce in one go).

■ Tell the children that each block has its special bed in the bedroom. Today they have been playing all day long and are so tired that they cannot find their beds. Ask the children to help all the Block People find their own comfortable beds.

■ Give each child a Bricks' Bedroom plan and the three bricks. Ask them to take one finger and trace any face of the brick; next trace this shape in the air, saying its name; and then choose the bed that matches this shape and put the brick to sleep on it.

■ Check that all the bricks are comfortable. They must match the plan exactly.

■ Continue the activity with as many different building blocks as you feel is appropriate.

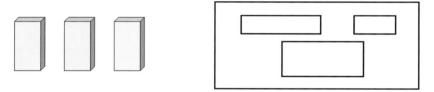

■ If necessary, show the children how to turn some of the blocks on their sides so that there is a block "sleeping comfortably in every bed on the plan."

■ Continue the activity with as many different building blocks as you feel is appropriate.

What Can I See from One Point of View?

■ Let the children build any structure they wish using the building blocks. When they have finished ask them to show you, which is the front-view (Camera Shot), the top-view (Bird's Eye View) and the side-view (Nosy Neighbour). They could point or they could pretend to perform the action (take a photo from the front for the front-view, stand on tiptoes arms outstretched and look down from above for the top-view, move to the right side of the table, wrinkle nose and peer for the side-view).

■ Ask the children to name all the blocks they can see, first from the front, then from the top, then from the side.

Tidy Up Time

■ At the end of the session, encourage the children to dismantle their structures, sort the blocks and put them away in the appropriate trays. Play an appropriate piece of music that the children will come to associate with clearing away. Promote willing participation by making a game of it.

SO MANY SLIDES
BUILDING ACCORDING TO A DETAILED DIAGRAM AND A GHOST DIAGRAM

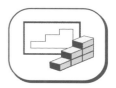

AIMS

- To practise analysing detailed diagrams of an object (slides).
- To practise identifying an object's main features, their functions, and the spatial relationship between them.
- To develop the ability to analyse slides visually and select the blocks required to build them.
- To practise building structures without detailed information.
- To develop the ability to transform a Ghost Diagram (2D outline of a slide) into a 3D structure (block slide).
- To foster self-regulation – plan the sequence of blocks required to build a slide and select appropriate blocks in the correct sequence.
- To develop creativity – the ability to design and build their own version of a structure (a slide).

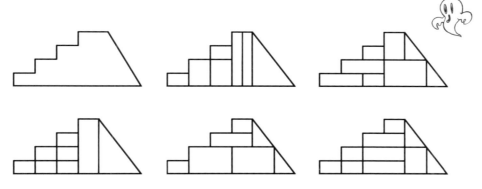

RESOURCES

For the teacher:
- ✓ 5 detailed diagrams of slides (2 sets).
- ✓ Additional building blocks for use by the children as required.
- ✓ 2D outline diagram of a slide, Stand for a diagram.

For each child:
- ✓ 2 x 1/2 cubes, 4 small triangular prisms, 1 long board, 2 x 1/2 cubes, 2 cubes, 2 cuboids and access to additional blocks as required.
- ✓ Ghost Diagram (2D outline) of a slide.

LEARNING OUTCOMES

- Children analyse a detailed diagram of a slide.
- Children analyse a Ghost Diagram of a slide.
- Children select the blocks required to build a version (or several versions) of a slide according to a Ghost Diagram.
- Children build a version (or several versions) of a slide according to a Ghost Diagram.   →

PROCEDURE

Camera Shot (Building According to Front-view Detailed Diagram)

- Show the children a full-sized front-view diagram of a slide.
- Fix it in an upright position (with its bottom edge touching the table).
- Analyse the different elements of the diagram with the children. Establish which building blocks will be required to build the slide. Discuss ways of ensuring that the blocks they plan to use are the correct size. Agree that when we choose a block it should exactly match its picture in the camera shot. Consequently, a good way to check is by placing each block we choose next to its picture and seeing if they do match.
- If necessary, model the building process. Ask children to help you choose bricks; match them to the camera shot; then build.
- Whether or not you decide to model the building process, make sure the children grasp the required sequence of actions. Look at the camera shot first; next choose the bricks; then check them one at a time against the camera shot (front-view diagram); finally build the slide.

- Children transform copies of a Ghost Diagram of a slide into different detailed diagrams.
- Children build 3D slides according to detailed 2D diagrams.
- Children design and build their own slides.

■ Give each child a construction basket. Give different camera shots (front-view diagrams) of slides to each child. Place the cards in stands so that they are vertical, rather than flat on the table.

Transformation (From Ghost Diagram to Detailed Diagram)

■ The aim of this type of activity is to enable children to regulate their own thinking processes. At first, the teacher supports the children by verbalising appropriate questions about the Ghost Diagram; with experience and learning, the children internalize the process and ask themselves these questions. They develop the ability to analyse any ghost diagram independently.

■ Show the children a Ghost Diagram of a slide. Focus on analysing the Ghost Diagram together. Ask questions to guide the process of analysis. E.g., what is this? Who uses it? What is it for? (A slide – children climb up steps on one side , slide down the other). Are we looking at a front, top or side-view? (A side-view). What are the component parts? (Steps, a platform and a slope). How could we build it? Which building blocks would we use for each part? How could we connect them?

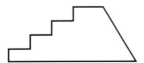 

■ Ask the children to think about how to transform the Ghost Diagram into a detailed diagram that shows which blocks they could use to build the slide. Use their suggestions to create a detailed diagram, drawing lines to show the position of the blocks with a dry-wipe marker.

■ Give each child a set of blocks. Ask them to build the slide according to the detailed diagram you have created together.

■ When they have completed this task, ask the children to build another slide of their own design; give them access to the additional blocks.

How Many Ways?

■ Tell the children that in a minute you will show them a Detailed Diagram of a slide. Their task is to take one look, then draw on a 2D Ghost Diagram the blocks they could use to fill it.

■ When everyone has drawn a detailed diagram based on the same Ghost Diagram, tell them you want to find out how many different ways there are to solve the mystery of the Ghost Diagram. Give the children access to as many as they wish.

■ Obviously, the children can draw many different detailed diagrams based on the same Ghost Diagram. Invite Ghost to float over the children's drawings to confirm that the children have based all their detailed diagrams on the same Ghost Diagram. Comment on Ghost's behalf, maybe, "I can't believe my eyes – Paul's drawing is different from Nikki's but they both solved my mystery! Yes, I can see that everyone has found a different solution to the mystery of my diagram. Well done!"

■ When Ghost has admired the detailed diagrams ask the children to design and build a new slide. Give out some play people and allow time for free play.

EXPLORATION

THROUGH GAMES, STORIES AND SIMPLE YET POWERFUL EXPERIMENTS CHILDREN DISCOVER IMPORTANT SCIENTIFIC CONCEPTS – STATES OF MATTER, DIFFERENT QUALITIES OF SUBSTANCES AND TRANSFORMATIONS

Overview	The Exploration programme introduces the children to important fundamental scientific concepts about themselves, the natural and material world and simple yet powerful experiments.
	It introduces children to ideas about opposites and about different properties of matter, for example textures (hard/soft); states of matter (liquid/solid?) the properties of air (it is everywhere, it is invisible, movements of air produce wind, it supports the flight of aeroplanes and birds, it exerts pressure); density (will an object sink or float?). It encourages children to look closely at everyday objects through a microscope.
Why are these skills important?	The programme helps children develop the ability to analyse changes or transformations from one state to another. The children study irreversible transformations. These include an introduction to processes of growth and maturation where the current state of a child, plant or animal reveals its past and/or future and to the cyclical transformation of the seasons. It also includes an introduction to concepts about the transformation of objects by human skill as well as to concepts about breaking objects and the implications this has. Some things cannot be returned to their original state and this has important consequences – ecological damage if we destroy trees, waste if we damage domestic artefacts and toys.
	They also learn about reversible transformations – water taking on the shape of its container; the three states of water and the processes of boiling, freezing, evaporating, condensing; the transformation of salt as it dissolves in water; the recovery of salt as water evaporates from a salt solution; the use of a thermometer to measure changes in temperature.
How does this programme work?	A key feature of the programme is the opportunity it offers young children to participate in simple experiments. They are able to observe transformations as they happen, to look carefully, to talk about what they have seen, and to think about the conditions that are necessary for the experiment to work. They have a chance to predict what will happen and to check their ideas against real outcomes.
	The most unusual feature of the programme is the innovative use of games and stories in exploring natural physical phenomena. These are at the heart of the programme. They have been carefully planned and structured to capture and retain the children's attention as well as to support them in actively building knowledge and understanding of different concepts and ideas.
The benefits of this programme	As in all the other Key to Learning programmes, opportunities to develop crucial thinking skills are embedded within the planned activities. The tasks set may call for symbolisation (e.g. a substitute shape, stylised drawing, or physical gesture to represent a state of matter); modelling (e.g. the use of a sequence of physical gestures to represent the temporal sequence as steam transforms first to water and then to ice as it cools); logical analysis (e.g. an invitation to predict what will happen next in an experiment and then check to see what actually happened); or creative production (e.g. the opportunity to solve a character's dilemma and explain why your solution works during discussion of the stories).

CONDENSATION

AIMS

- To introduce the concept of water condensation – steam turns into water as it cools.

SAFETY NOTES

- The activities described in this session are designed to provide a memorable learning experience, and have all been carried out successfully with young children. However, you will need to check that any activities carried out with young children in your own setting minimise risks and comply with your own health and safety policies.
- Take care when holding the mirror above the steam.
- Ensure that the children do not come into contact with the hot kettle, and that they understand that steam can cause injury.

PROCEDURE

- Use questions to help the children remember what they know about evaporation (heat turns liquid water into steam, in cold weather water turns into snow/ice).
- Tell the story of Masha and the Witch. Use the pictures at appropriate points to keep them focussed.

"Once upon a time, a young girl called Masha went mushroom picking in the forest. The sun shone brightly. It was very hot, as it so often is in the summer. It wasn't at all like cold frosty winter when your breath comes out in mists. Masha spent such a long time picking mushrooms that she grew very thirsty. However, there was no water nearby. Masha was so thirsty that she began to long for the icy winter when there is plenty of snow everywhere. If she wanted a drink in the winter she could...what could she do? Yes, she could melt some snow in her hands or her mouth, and turn it into water to satisfy her thirst. But it was the middle of summer and there was no snow.

Masha searched for a stream – in those days you could usually a find a stream of clean water to drink from in the forest. But today, she could not find a stream anywhere. Suddenly, out of nowhere she saw

RESOURCES

For the teacher:
- ✓ Boiling water in a kettle or a pot.
- ✓ A mirror or a piece of glass.
- ✓ Pictures – the Witch's house, the Witch, Masha, a stream in the forest.
- ✓ Story – Masha and the Witch.

LEARNING OUTCOMES

- Children know that steam condenses i.e. it becomes liquid water when it cools.
- Children know that steam transforms into water when it comes into contact with something cold.

a hut in a little clearing in the forest. The door of the hut was open, but Masha was a polite child, so she knocked before she went in. It was a witch's hut.

Masha realised this as soon as she saw the witch! But Masha was very brave and she did not let that frighten her. "Good afternoon," she said to the Witch.

"Good afternoon, Masha", the Witch replied. "Why have you come?"

"I'm so thirsty," said Masha. "Won't you please give me a glass of water?"

The Witch was very crafty. She decided to test Masha. In the middle of the hut there stood a huge stove with a huge cauldron full of water on it. The Witch lit a hot fire. Soon the water in the cauldron was bubbling, hissing and boiling fiercely. Hot white steam rose up into the air. *(Boil the kettle; let the children watch steam rising).*

The Witch looked at Masha slyly. "So you want a drink of water do you?" she said. "Well I know a beautiful little stream of cool clear water, and I will show you where it is. But first you must solve my puzzle. And if you can't you must stay here forever and pick mushrooms for me! The puzzle is – drink a glass of water from my hissing cauldron!" Masha looked at the cauldron with the clouds of steam rising from it. The water was far too hot! Masha knew that if she tried to drink that water her tongue

would blister and burn. But she was so thirsty. And she did not want to stay with the Witch forever, picking mushrooms! Masha thought carefully and then she....do you know what she did? *(Ask for ideas).*

"If the water is too hot, and I need to drink some, then I must cool it down!" thought Masha.

Now Masha always kept a little mirror in her bag. Masha touched the mirror. It was just as she thought. The mirror's surface was cold. *(Let the children touch the cool surface of a mirror.)*

"That's it!" thought Masha. "I can't drink the boiling water. And if I try to put some in a glass I will scald my hands. However, steam turns into water when it cools! And I can cool the steam, if I am very careful. All I have to do is hold my mirror up to the steam. When the steam touches my cold mirror, it will turn back into water. Then I can collect the water in the Witch's glass."

And that is what Masha did. Working very carefully – for after all she did not want the boiling water or the hot steam to scald her – Masha held her cold mirror up to the steam. As the steam touched her mirror it turned into drops of water. The drops of water ran down the mirror, and Masha collected them in the Witch's glass *(Use steam from the kettle, a cold mirror, and a glass to demonstrate how Masha condensed water from steam and collected the water drops in a glass).*

The Witch was shocked, but she had to keep her promise. "You are a clever girl, Masha," she said. "You have outwitted me! Now I will show you the stream".

The Witch showed Masha a beautiful little stream of cool clear water, and Masha drank her fill. Then the Witch gave Masha some berries and extra mushrooms to put in her bag. What a good thing it was that Masha had a cold mirror in her bag. And what a good thing it was that she knew how to use it to turn steam into water. And if ever you should meet a sly Witch who asks difficult puzzles, I do hope that you will remember too."

- When the witch shows Masha the cauldron of boiling water, show the children steam coming from a kettle of boiling water; remind them that steam is very hot and will scald if they touch it.

- When Masha takes out her mirror, let the children touch a mirror to establish that it is cold.

- Use the mirror to demonstrate how Masha condensed and collected water from the steam.

- At the end of the story, ask questions to make sure the children have understood the key point; steam turns into water when we cool it.

PLAYING WITH SYMBOLS:
ICE – WATER – STEAM

AIM

- To consolidate knowledge of the three states of water.
- To introduce symbols for ice, water, steam, warmth and cold.
- To practise understanding and using the symbols.

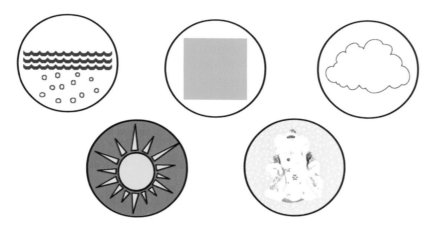

RESOURCES

For the teacher:

✓ Set of symbols.

✓ Blue cardboard square – representing ice.

✓ White cardboard circle with waves and bubbles – representing water.

✓ Piece of white cardboard cut out in the shape of a cloud – representing steam.

✓ A cardboard circle with the picture of Father Frost on a background of snowflakes – representing cold.

✓ A cardboard circle with a picture of the yellow sun with rays on a red background – representing heat.

✓ Extracts of music representing ice (slow music in minor key), water (active, lively music) and steam (light, fast music) e.g. fragments from the ballet "Hunchbacked Horse" by R. Schedrin: ice – "Night" fragment; water – "Gold fish"; steam – "Swimming in the cauldrons".

PROCEDURE

Solid – Liquid

■ The children stand in a circle and follow verbal instructions.

Instruction	Action
Cold, ice!	*Hold hands close to the body and shiver*
Warm, ice melts and turns into water!	*Pretend to swim*
Hot, water turns into steam!	*Circle arms in the air and hiss*
Cold, steam turns back into water!	*Pretend to swim*
Freezing, water turns into ice!	*Hold hands close to the body and shiver*

■ Tell the children they are going to play the game again, but this time special cards will tell them what to do.

■ Discuss the symbol cards for heat and cold, using questions to help the children make the connection between the symbol, the processes represented, and the required actions.

■ Play several rounds of the game showing first one of the symbol cards then the other while the children transform from ice to water, from water to steam, from steam to water, and back to ice again Continue to give verbal instructions: "Heat! Ice turns to water! Swim!" "Hot! Water turns to steam! Hiss!" "Cold! Steam turns to water! Swim!" "Cold! Water turns to ice! Shiver!".

■ Now tell the children that they are going to play the game without anyone using any words at all.

LEARNING OUTCOMES

- Children know the effect of cold on steam and water.

- Children know the effect of heat on ice and water.   →

- Children recognise that specific images may represent ice, water, steam, heat and cold.
- Children respond with appropriate actions to cards representing the action of heat on ice and water.
- Children respond with appropriate actions to cards representing the action of cold on steam and water.

Symbol Card	Process represented	Action
Heat: yellow sun with rays on a red background 	A heat source transforms ice into water, water into steam	Pretend to swim Unless the card changes, circle hands and hiss
Cold: Father Frost on a background of snowflakes 	Cold transforms steam to water, water to ice	Pretend to swim Unless the card changes, hold hands close to the body and shiver

■ Show the children the symbols for ice, water and steam; use questions to help the children recognise what each symbol represents (the blue square looks like hard, cold ice; the waves and bubbles look like water, the white fluffy cloud looks like steam).

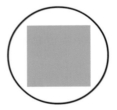 

■ Play the game again using the symbols to prompt the children's actions – if necessary provide verbal prompts until the children get it!

■ You may wish to extend the game by asking a child to give the instructions.

■ You may wish to play the game again using appropriate musical themes to represent ice, water and steam.

■ You may wish to end the session by having the children draw their own representations of water, ice and steam.

PROPERTIES OF SUBSTANCES

AIMS

- To know that when we break solid objects, we cannot restore them to their original state.
- To know that if we pour a liquid into different containers, we can return it unchanged to its original container.
- To develop an understanding of consequences – ecological (we cannot repair trees if we damage them) and domestic (damaged objects can be repaired but not restored to their original state).

PROCEDURE

- Give out the sticks and talk to the children about their properties. Use questions to establish that the sticks are hard, solid, and make a noise when you bang them on the table or together.
- Point out that the children have one stick each; ask them to break their sticks, and establish that each child now has two sticks.
- Ask the children to find out if they can put the sticks together again to make one stick; get them to agree that it is not possible.
- Repeat this process with the chalk. Get the children to tell you what the stick and the chalk have in common, using questions to guide and prompt the discussion (they are both solid, and if broken can not be put back together again). Generalise to other solid objects, e.g. toys, windows etc.
- Now generalise natural and everyday objects, e.g. trees and toys. Explain that trees may not recover and this is why it is important not to damage them; emphasise that damage to toys may make the toys unusable and the owner very sad.
- You may wish to end this part of the session by singing "Humpty Dumpty" whilst you gather up the sticks and chalk.
- Now ask the children if it is possible to break a piece of ice into smaller pieces. Break the ice, and ask if it is possible to put the pieces back together.
- Get the children to try; get them to agree that it is not possible – ice is solid, and once broken the pieces won't fit together.
- Ask the children how we might break up some water – after you have listened to their ideas, give each child a glass of water and an empty

RESOURCES

For the teacher:
- ✓ Piece of ice, water, cube.
- ✓ Large container for water; other containers in different sizes and shapes.

For each child:
- ✓ Wooden stick, piece of chalk.
- ✓ Bar of plasticine.
- ✓ Glass of water.
- ✓ Empty glass.

LEARNING OUTCOMES

- Children know that they cannot put solid objects together again if they break them.
- Children know that they can separate liquids, and then put the parts together again.
- Children understand that breaking solid objects has physical and sometimes emotional consequences; damaged solid objects cannot be restored to their original state and this sometimes causes unhappiness.

glass. Show the children how to "break" their water by pouring some of it into the empty glass, so that they end up with two "pieces" of water.

■ Next have them pour the water back into one glass – now they have one "piece" of water again. Remind them that water is not solid, but liquid.

■ Ask for other examples of liquids (juice, soup, milk etc.). Explain that we can "break" any liquid and then make it "whole" again.

■ Show the children that they can make one "big water" from all their "little waters", by pouring all the water from the glasses into a big container.

■ Clear away the water and the glasses, and then give each child a bar of plasticine. Talk to the children about the plasticine, using questions and instructions to prompt and guide the discussion (the plasticine is solid, hard and cold, when we use our hands to warm it, the plasticine becomes soft, warm, and can be rolled out into a thin, flat shape).

■ Ask the children to "break" their plasticine into two pieces; then have the children put the two pieces together again. Explain that now the plasticine is soft it can be broken and put back together again.

■ Talk about the properties of solids (they are hard, we can't pour them, they stay the same shape unless we break them, we cannot put them together again if we break them).

■ Show the children that liquids change shape very easily. Pour water into a variety of differently shaped containers, e.g. a deep bowl, a shallow bowl, a square fish tank, etc. Put a cube into the same containers and point out that it does not change its shape.

■ End by reminding the children that when we break solids we cannot put them back the way they were.

■ You may wish to end with a suitable story or poem about something getting broken.

■ Over the following week, help the children to make links between the session and everyday experience; draw their attention to broken toys; allow them to help you mend damaged items. Point out that we can still see that the object has been broken even after we have repaired it.

EXPRESSIVE MOVEMENT

**DEVELOPS EMOTIONAL INTELLIGENCE, NON-VERBAL COMMUNICATION
SKILLS, CREATIVITY AND PRODUCTIVE IMAGINATION
THROUGH BODY MOVEMENT, GESTURES,
FACIAL EXPRESSIONS AND MUSIC**

Overview

This programme offers young children the opportunity to develop emotional intelligence and non-verbal communication skills with the help of movement, gestures and expression.

It fosters creativity, asking children to use their bodies to produce their own imaginative representations of emotional states, animals, people, and scenarios.

Why are these skills important?

The importance of non-verbal communication and expressive movement is unquestionable.

Babies begin to use non-verbal language from the moment they are born. Even before they can speak they have started to make use of the system of non-verbal signals, the language of facial expression, posture, gesture, gaze and personal space that they will use for effective communication in everyday life. Posture and facial expression also encode our emotions. It is one way we convey important information about ourselves to others. Some basic emotions are difficult to conceal, even if we wish to conceal them, and there are few emotions or feelings which cannot be expressed by movements of the body.

We can acquire a measure of conscious control of non-verbal communication through self awareness, knowledge and understanding. Learning to "read" others and to move our own bodies expressively is fundamental to the development of emotional intelligence.

How does this programme work?

The Expressive Movement programme includes activities to help children acquire a rich repertoire of gestures that they can use in communicating with both adults and peers. They learn socially acceptable ways to express needs, desires and mood. They learn to mimic intonation, posture, stance, and gait. They learn to vary speed of movement, tension/relaxation of muscles and tempo of breathing. They learn to use this vocabulary of movement to produce their own imaginative responses to a variety of tasks. They learn how to work together to perform in front of an audience; they also learn how a good audience responds.

These tasks provide opportunities to develop self-regulation, self-confidence and self-awareness; to learn how to work with others; to acquire the skills required for "reading" feelings, moods, and attitudes; and to develop creativity through the production of imaginative performance.

A key feature of the programme is that it is highly active. Young children are naturally kinaesthetic learners, and consequently find the programme particularly easy to access. Another important feature of the programme is the use of music. There are a range of tasks which introduce young children to some of the ways in which the use of sound, rhythm and melody can set, enhance or alter mood.

The benefits of this programme

Like all the Key to Learning programmes, Expressive Movement deliberately and systematically fosters the development of key cognitive processes. The programme involves four key cognitive processes: symbolisation (e.g. the use of gesture to encode meaning); visual modelling (e.g. learning through mimicry, expressing ideas through sequences of movement); logical analysis (e.g. considering which features of bodily expression provide the best match for expressing a given aspect of behaviour); and creative self-expression.

TALKING TO BIRD

AIMS

- To understand the meaning of a variety of gestures (greeting, beckoning a friend, offering food, waving goodbye, nodding in agreement).
- To use the gestures to interact with a puppet.
- To introduce a technique for imitating the actions of a bird.
- To develop vocal mimicry – using a clear, long drawn-out sound.

PROCEDURE

Talking to Bird

- Have the children sit in a semicircle on chairs; ensure the chairs have spaces between them.
- Tell the children that Bird has arrived to visit them, but if they want to see her they will have to call for her. Show the children how to place their hands in front of their mouths to form a loudspeaker. Call "B-i-ird!" using a clear ringing tone, and long drawn out vowel sound. Ask the children to call with you.
- Explain that Bird is shy and will not come out. Ask for ideas to encourage Bird to come out.
- Show the children how to summon Bird – stretch out a hand gently, palm upwards, and beckon with your index finger. Explain that it is very important to look straight at Bird if we want to call her: we always look at our friends when we talk to them.
- Encourage the children to copy this gesture several times, and to say expressively: "Come here please, Bird, come here!"
- When the children have complied, have Bird approach the children and bow.
- Ask the children why Bird bowed (Bird wanted to greet us but can only talk by using gestures)
- Ask the children to return the bow, and then show the children how to feed Bird.
- Help the children "feed Bird"; they get some imaginary grain, hold it in an outstretched hand and offer it to Bird. Have Bird "peck" gently at the "grains" on the outstretched hands. Reassure fearful children, but if a child still does not want to feed Bird say, "Maybe next time."

Bird Flaps her Wings and Sings

- Place the puppet where it can "watch" the children, then ask the children to stand up and imagine that they are little birds; they must "flap their wings" (move outstretched arms up and down) and sing like Bird, i.e. sing "Tweet-tweet" in a clear ringing tone, emphasising the sound of the vowel.
- Ask the children to sit down again, bring out the puppet, and discuss the children's work. Have Bird confirm that "the children were excellent – they sounded just like me!"
- Tell the children it is time for Bird to go, and introduce a ritual for departing guests e.g. thank the guest for coming, invite the guest to come again, have the guest accept the invitation, exchange polite bows, agree that the guest will come again, wave as you say goodbye.

RESOURCES

For the teacher:
- ✓ Hand puppet – Bird.
- ✓ Place for Bird to sit.

LEARNING OUTCOMES

- Children recognise and use a variety of basic communicative gestures to interact with a hand puppet – greet (nod), beckon, offer food, bow and wave goodbye.
- Children look directly at the puppet when they "talk" to it.
- Children imitate a summoning call (B-i-ird!) and bird song (Tweet-tweet).

RESOURCES

For the teacher:
✓ Toy car.

LEARNING OUTCOMES

- Children pretend to drive a car.
- Children stop when the teacher says, "Stop."
- Children start when the teacher says, "Let's go."

LET'S DRIVE THE CAR

AIMS

- To enter into the emotional and imaginative world of a story through movement.
- To develop a rich repertoire of expressive actions.
- To copy the teacher's changes of expressive action.
- To start performing an action in response to a verbal or non verbal request.
- To stop performing an action in response to a verbal or non verbal request.

PROCEDURE

Let's Stamp on the Brakes

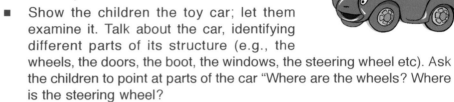

- Show the children the toy car; let them examine it. Talk about the car, identifying different parts of its structure (e.g., the wheels, the doors, the boot, the windows, the steering wheel etc). Ask the children to point at parts of the car "Where are the wheels? Where is the steering wheel?

- You might like to sing an appropriate action song about a car.

- Tell the children that they are going to pretend to drive a car, but first they have to learn to make the car start.

- Say, "We have to switch on the engine." Imitate turning on the ignition (e.g. pretend to turn on the switch and say "Click click") then make an engine noise. Encourage the children to copy you.

- Say, "And we're off!" Continue making the engine noises, varying the volume and intensity to maintain interest; as you do this pretend to steer.

- Say, "Sometimes when we are out driving we have to stop our cars very quickly – maybe we see a rabbit in the road and if we don't stop we'll hit it! We have to stamp on the brakes with our foot very quickly, like this". Show the children how to "stamp on the brakes" i.e. stamp your right foot hard.

- Say, "Let's see if we can all stop our cars very quickly. When I say "Stop!" stamp on your brakes. And – stop! "

- "Stamp on your brake" as you say "Stop!" Praise the children who copy you. (If you are the only one to "stamp on the brake" say, "Well I stamped on my brake! Let's try again!").

- Say, "Let's go!" and encourage the children to copy you as you make engine noises and "steer."

- Repeat the sequence of driving and saying stop; praise children as they follow your instructions, to provide positive feedback for those who comply and also to encourage those who have not yet complied to follow suit.

- To help avoid accidents remember to keep checking that the children are well spaced out – the cars must not be too close together or they might crash. You may wish to end the session by following the routine for saying goodbye to a visitor (the car).

FRIGHTENED FOREST CREATURES AND THE DANGEROUS WOLVES

AIMS

- To develop expressive movements for conveying kindness, unkindness and sadness (longing).
- To combine these movements with expressive movements for representing a specific character.
- To practise staying in role while working directly with a partner (teacher/peer).
- To move freely and fluently using the whole body.

PROCEDURE

Warm Up to Music or to Rhythm

- Instructions might include
    - Walk around the classroom swinging your arms, alternating slow pace and fast steps.
    - Spring gently on both legs; gradually start to jump (both legs); hop from one leg to the other; then hop on one leg, then the other; jog slowly round the room, pick up speed.
    - Sway from one leg to the other: sway backwards and forwards and from side to side; swing arms in the same direction as the sway.
    - Jog around the room, spin and change direction.
    - Run on tiptoes around the room with arms to the sides.
    - Free improvisation – choose your own movements (e.g. sway, spin, run lightly etc.)

Angry Unkind Wolf

- Explain that the wolf is in a bad mood. S/he is feeling angry and is being unkind.
- Use expressive movements to imitate an angry and aggressive wolf; bend forwards a little; move around the room on slightly bent legs, using soft steps; arms tight for a "closed" body; tightly hunched shoulders; a glowering expression, jaw jutting out, teeth bared in a fierce grin; hands held like "paws" with "claws" out.
- Practise together, encouraging the children to move expressively, using the whole body. Perform the movements to the music chosen for the angry unkind wolf.

Dangerous Wolves!

- Help the children to find and practise expressive movements for representing a wolf menacing another animal, e.g. use hands with fingers held to resemble claws to swipe the air.
- Show the children how to work with a partner when pretending to be a wolf menacing another animal. Choose a child as your partner.

RESOURCES

For the teacher:

✓ CD player or tape recorder, music for Warm Up.

✓ Music to accompany the wolf performances, e.g. excerpts from the wolf theme from "Peter and the Wolf" by S. Prokofiev.

✓ Pictures of angry wolf and lonely wolf for illustration (optional).

LEARNING OUTCOMES

- Children use expressive movements to pretend to be unkind and kind whilst using expressive movements for imitating a wolf.
- Children pretend to be frightened forest animals.
- Children stay in role whilst working with a partner (pretend to be attacking wolves).
- Children show some ability to move freely and fluently, using the whole body.

- Explain that you are standing far enough away from your partner to ensure that you will not touch him/her when you pretend to menace him/her; pretend to menace your partner and show how you swipe the air with your claws, but never come close enough to touch.

- Divide the children into pairs. Show them how to check for a safe distance – stretch out your arms to make sure they do not reach your partner before you begin the game.

- Have the children take it in turns to pretend to be the dangerous wolf, swiping at but never touching their partner.

- Divide into two groups; the "dangerous wolves" and the "frightened forest creatures". The forest animals freeze in position in the forest; the angry dangerous wolves prowl between them; when a "dangerous wolf" comes close to a forest creature it pretends to swipe without ever touching. Emphasis that the "dangerous wolves" are not allowed to touch the "forest creatures").

- Practise, then have the groups change places so that the "forest animals" are now "dangerous wolves", and vice versa. Practise again.

- Now perform to the chosen music, letting all the children have a turn at being "dangerous wolves" and "forest creatures."

Frightened Forest Creatures

- Show the children how to pretend to be animals that are frightened by a dangerous wolf; huddle, squat or run away and hide, cover your head with your hands, clutch your mouth, and widen your eyes with fear.

- Encourage the children to perform all the movements; praise children who perform the movements expressively and precisely, being as specific as possible about what they are doing well (this should help those who get it right to be clear about what they are doing well and encourage others to imitate them).

Sad, Lonely Wolf

- Explain that the wolf has been so unkind that no one wants to be friends with him/her. The wolf is "very lonely" and feels sad.

- Show the children expressive movements for representing a sad lonely wolf; walk slowly around the room, head down, sad expression; stop periodically, raise your head, stretch your neck and howl mournfully like a wolf; sit down and pretend to cry, muttering in a low voice "I'm all alone and nobody wants to be my friend; I'm so sad and lonely."

- Perform these actions together.

Learning to be Kind

- Remind the children that the wolf feels very sad because s/he is lonely; s/he has no friends and nobody wants to play with him/her.

- Ask the children to tell you why no one wants to be friends with the wolf and what he could do to make friends.

- Tell the children that when the wolf stopped crying, s/he realised that if s/he wanted to make friends she would have to stop being unkind.

- Ask the children to be very kind wolves: let them practise, then if necessary join in and show them some expressive movements for representing kind wolves; run lightly around the room, with an "open" body, and heads up. Perform these movements to the chosen music.

- Finally, ask the children to show how the kind wolf treats other animals; s/he touches gently, s/he strokes, s/he shares food etc.

- Ask some of the children to pretend to be forest creatures; the others pretend to be the wolf treating them kindly.

- Pretend to be a forest animal and let the "wolves" take it in turn to treat you kindly.

YOU – ME – WORLD

USING SYMBOLS AND VISUAL MODELS CHILDREN LEARN ABOUT THEMSELVES AS PHYSICAL, EMOTIONAL AND SOCIAL BEINGS; ABOUT THE NATURAL AND MATERIAL WORLD; ABOUT LIVING THINGS AND INANIMATE OBJECTS

Overview

This programme offers young children the opportunity to learn about themselves as physical, emotional and social beings. They learn about the natural and material world, about living things and inanimate objects, and about relationships between people. They are encouraged to explore, to empathise and to help others learn.

Why are these skills important?

Babies and young children are programmed from birth to respond to the varied and astonishing sensory stimulation provided by their natural environment. By the time they reach pre-school, what they have already discovered about the world prompts a phase of intense questioning. Why? Why do birds fly away or leaves fall down? Why do we have to wear coats in winter? Where do animals sleep? What are things made of? What happens to our food when we eat?

How does this programme work?

By taking advantage of this natural curiosity about their social and physical surroundings, the programme provides a rich set of resources for helping young children to structure and extend the understanding of their immediate environment and of salient relationships in the natural world. It helps to foster curiosity and keep it alive. It also helps to foster respect for the natural world, laying an early foundation upon which children will later be able to build a more sophisticated (and increasingly essential) understanding of environmental and ecological issues.

A sense of security, of familiarity, of being known and valued is the necessary foundation for a happy and successful introduction to learning. However, to be able to benefit from opportunities to learn in a group, young children also need opportunities to develop the skills required for group work. At the most basic level, they need self awareness and awareness of others. They need to know what they are feeling and they need the ability to recognise what others feel. Hence, the programme opens with work aimed at helping children to feel valued, familiarising them with their setting, and establishing ground rules for behaviour before moving on to work aimed at developing self-awareness, the ability to name and recognise emotional expressions.

The topics gradually widen their focus with work to develop understanding the local environment and road safety. Other topics focus on information and concepts about families and family relationships; about animals, plants and the materials used to make everyday objects; about the body and its workings; about time, the weather and the seasons.

The benefits of this programme

Like all the other Key to Learning programmes, You-Me-World aims to help children develop their knowledge and understanding. At the same time, it deliberately and systematically employs the key cognitive processes of symbolisation, modelling, logical analysis and creative self-expression which are required for the development of cognitive abilities.

Teachers working within the framework set by the DFES Curriculum Guidance for the Foundation Stage will find that You-Me-World provides structured opportunities to focus on foundation stage goals within the areas of Personal, Social and Emotional Wellbeing and of Knowledge and Understanding of the World. There are also ample opportunities for young children to develop skills in communication and mathematical language (time).

WHO LIVES HERE?

AIMS

- To develop the ability to use symbols to represent an adult and a child.
- To develop the ability to construct representations of a house and family.
- To use representations of a house and a family.
- To develop the concept of "an address".
- To learn their address – the number of the house and the name of the road.
- To develop the ability to use substitute shapes to represent real objects.

RESOURCES

For the teacher:

✓ Pictures of the bear family.

✓ Large and small circles.

✓ List of children's addresses.

For the children:

✓ A4 representation of a house.

✓ Glue stick.

✓ Small plastic cup (with lid).

 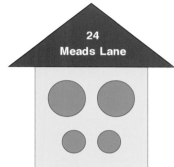

PROCEDURE

- Before the session, ask parents to help you familiarise the children with their addresses (number and road name).

- Have Teddy visit, show pictures of the bear family and talk about them; have Teddy ask the children questions about their families. Explain that Teddy wants to tell his family everything the children have said, but is worried because he cannot remember it all.

- Show the children how Teddy can use large and small circles to help him remember. Establish that Teddy can use big circles to represent the adults in a family and small circles for the children. Give each child a sheet of paper with a house on it and a glue stick; help the children choose appropriate circles for each member of their own households and stick them.

- Have the children use their representation to tell Teddy about their families; have Teddy ask each child for their address ("in case I want to visit you"). Write the address on the paper as the child gives Teddy the information; have the list of addresses ready in case the children need help; give Teddy the representations to "take back home to the forest".

- Help each child make a special reminder of his/her address. Use small plastic cups with lids ("your house"); display the child's name prominently on the side (e.g. Jack's House). Help each child put large and small circles into the cup to represent every member of his/her household. Ask them individually to tell you their house number and the name of their road; using sticky labels, write this information on the top of each cup. Tell the children that they can use their special cups to show visitors their addresses.

LEARNING OUTCOMES

- Children use symbols to represent adult and child members of their household.

- Children recognise a representation of a house and family.

- Children give their address – the number of the house and the name of the road.

RESOURCES

For the teacher:

✓ Pictures of plants and animals.

✓ Pictures of inanimate objects.

✓ 2 schematic drawings of houses (A4 or A3 if possible).

✓ Symbolic drawing to represent the category "plants".

✓ Symbolic drawing to represent the category "animals".

✓ Plant.

LEARNING OUTCOMES

· Children differentiate between living and non-living things.

· Children classify living things as plants or animals.

· Children classify animals as meat eaters or as plant eaters.

PLANTS AND ANIMALS

AIMS

● To develop the ability to distinguish between living (animate) and nonliving (inanimate) things.

● To develop the ability to distinguish between plants and animals.

● To practise using substitute signs and symbols to represent real objects.

● To foster the pleasure of connecting with nature.

● To introduce the concept of classification -use specified categories to group living things.

PROCEDURE

Alive – Not Alive

■ Spread all the pictures (objects, plants, animals) on the floor and help the children group them into two families; living things (animate) and non-living things (inanimate).

■ Now play "Alive/Not alive." Name a picture that belongs to one of the families. If it is alive, the children jump; if it is not alive they stand still.

Plants and Animals

- Take away all the pictures of inanimate objects. Spread the pictures of the plants and animals on the floor and ask the children what they all have in common. If necessary, remind them that these are pictures of living things (animate).

- Put out the schematic drawings of the houses. Ask two or three children to divide the living things into two families. Let the children work independently if possible; however, if the children do not categorise the pictures appropriately, explain that biologists (people who study living things) group all the plants in one family and all the animals in the other; encourage the children to classify the images in this way.

- Ask the children to help you create symbols for the plant family and the animal family house. Let them make suggestions and choose the best ones. Alternatively show them how to draw appropriate symbols. Place each symbol next to the correct house.

- Make two flags; put the animal symbol on one of the flags and the plant symbol on the other. Shuffle the pictures and then have the children help you place all the pictures in "Plant land" or "Animal land".

- Ask the children about the differences between the "inhabitants" of plant land and animal land.

- In the course of your discussion help the children reach the following conclusions:
  - Plants make their food themselves, using their leaves; they need sunshine, air and water to do this.
  - Animals cannot make their own food.

- Take all the animal pictures and talk about what the different animals eat. Note that some eat only plants but some eat other animals.

- Divide the animals into two categories (two animal families) with plant eaters (herbivores) in one family and meat eaters (carnivores) in the other.

- Talk about what people can eat – both meat and plants (omnivores).

- You may need or wish to acknowledge that many people choose not to eat meat, for religious or personal reasons.

Living Together

- Mix up all the living things picture cards and put them face down on the table. Ask each child in turn to turn over two cards.

- Ask the child to say,
  - The name of the living thing.
  - Whether it is a plant or an animal.
  - If it is an animal, whether it is a meat eater or a plant eater.
  - Whether or not one would eat the other, and if so which would eat which?

RESOURCES

For the teacher:

✓ Toy owl and stories/ poems that describe evening and night-time.

✓ Night Symbol Card, pictures of evening and night-time activities.

LEARNING OUTCOMES

• Children can talk about evening routines.

• Children can help owl go to sleep.

NIGHT TIME

AIMS

● To develop a sense of time.

● To develop knowledge and understanding of bedtime routines.

● To develop nurturing behaviour through pretend play (help Owl go to sleep).

PROCEDURE

■ If possible, read "Owl Babies" by Martin Waddell and Patrick Benson before the session. Introduce Owl to the children and explain that she has come to visit the preschool. (If the children have read "Owl Babies" you can introduce the toy owl as Mother Owl from the story.

■ Explain that Owl is nocturnal; this means she is a night bird. She wakes when we go to bed and stays awake during the night. That is why Owl can tell us what happens in the evenings and at night. Have Owl say, "Usually I'm asleep at this time of the day. I stayed awake especially to see you. When the sun goes down it becomes dark, and the moon and the stars appear in the sky, that is when I wake up. It is hard for children to see in the dark, but I have special eyes. My eyes help me to see when there is very little light. And a good thing too, because night is when I go hunting for my food. My special eyes help me to catch my food."

■ At this point, put a symbol card showing the moon and stars in the middle of the display board. Tell the children, that the card shows it is evening/night – the card represents night.

■ Have Owl ask the children to tell her what they do in the evenings and at night (e.g. Come home from preschool, have tea/dinner, watch some children's programmes, listen to a story, have a bath, brush teeth, go to bed). Talk about the activities the children name; where possible, focus on how the different activities meet the children's needs: for food, cleanliness, fun, closeness, sharing and relaxation.

■ If a child names an activity that is shown on one of the prepared pictures give him/her the picture and some blu-tak. Ask the child to fix the card near the night-time symbol (the picture of the moon and stars already on display). If a child names an activity for which you have no picture do a quick drawing on some spare card then ask the child to place it on the board.

■ Now have Owl ask the children what happens when it gets to be bedtime. Who tells them to go to bed? What does that person usually say? What do they usually say? Do they take special toys to bed? Do they say goodnight to the toys? Etc.

■ Play "It's Bedtime". Have the Owl pretend to get very sleepy. Explain that Owl really must go to bed now or she'll be too sleepy to get up and go hunting when it gets dark. Ask the children to help Owl go to sleep. Sing a lullaby to the Owl together, and then read some stories/ poems about evening and night to her. Pretend that Owl has fallen asleep. Let the children touch owl and say "Goodnight, sweet dreams" very tenderly, before tucking the toy up in some kind of bed/nest/box.

PARENT POWER
STRATEGIES FOR BUILDING
A POSITIVE PARTNERSHIP

It is our responsibility to take the parents with us on the learning journey.

Olga Dyachenko

- **ALL WORK AND NO PLAY**

- **IT'S NEVER TOO LATE TO LEARN, IT'S NEVER TOO EARLY TO TEACH**

- **"HOMEWORK" FOR PARENTS**

Mum, this is a very interesting school. It is not a school of answers; it is a school of questions! Gareth aged 4 (after spending 2 months at a Key to Learning preschool)

Early Years practitioners understand the importance of involving parents in the education of young children. Parents love and care for their children. This gives them three distinct advantages as partners in the education process. They know their children very well as individuals. They have the most powerful motivation possible for helping their children to learn. They are also eager to do things to help, particularly when their children are young.

However, it may not always be easy to translate parents' commitment to their children's education into support for an innovative curriculum.

All children are born geniuses, and we spend the first six years of their lives degeniusing them.
Buckminister Fuller

ALL WORK AND NO PLAY

Parents are bombarded with invitations to buy games and materials that are marketed as educational toys. Many of these are poor value for money because they offer closed tasks that are completed once and then discarded. Others "teach" letters and numbers prematurely in ways that are both boring and unhelpful. Such products also come to exert a disproportionate influence on parents' ideas about what constitutes good educational practice.

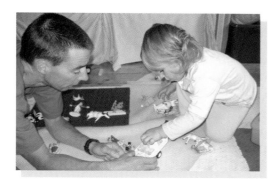

Conversely, many good parents underestimate the importance of lifestyle and active parenting. They may undervalue the significance of bedtime stories and messy play; of going for walks and outings; of talking together; and of limiting TV to suitable programmes that are watched and talked about with an adult.

Equally, many good parents do not find relaxed and playful interaction with their children easy or instinctive. They are often short of time and ideas. They may underestimate how much a short burst of high quality interaction can achieve, and how easy, pleasurable and satisfying it can be.

Finally, in countries like the UK, formal teaching starts early and so does formal testing. This prompts parents to focus on the importance of teaching children the basic skills of reading, writing and numeracy.

Parents may require a lot of reassurance that vital skills are not being neglected and that the Key to Learning Curriculum will effectively prepare their children for academic success and for happy and fulfilling lives.

IT'S NEVER TOO LATE TO LEARN,
IT'S NEVER TOO EARLY TO TEACH

It can be very helpful to hold meetings with parents to introduce them to Key to Learning. An initial meeting can provide parents with an opportunity to look at the materials. Practitioners can explain that the programmes aim to develop learning abilities, and encourage parents to ask questions.

From the new-born baby to the five year old is a chasm.
From the five year old to me is just one step.
Leo Tolstoy

Later on, parents often enjoy "It's never too late to learn, it's never too early to teach" sessions where the children teach them some of the Key to Learning games they have been playing.

These meetings also provide opportunities to explain the use of external mediators or visual reminders, e.g. writing rings that help a child remember the correct way to hold a pencil.

"HOMEWORK" FOR PARENTS

Another very important way of communicating with parents is through the Ideas for Parents activities pack. Teachers can simply provide parents with the whole pack, or provide them with activities from the pack that are relevant to this week's work, e.g. by making a stack of photocopies available in the parents' area.

The pack offers a number of significant benefits. It keeps parents informed about the work their children are doing during Key to Learning sessions. It prepares parents for the long words their children will be using (structure, parallelogram) and the thought provoking questions they are likely to start asking (What is the opposite of a chicken? Where does the wind come from?).

Most importantly, it provides parents with practical ways to become actively involved in their children's learning, through enjoyable games and activities linked to every aspect of the Key to Learning curriculum. Many of the activities can be carried out with no equipment, while walking a child to school or driving to the shops. All reinforce work that has been carried out in class.

Ideally, however, teachers will make use of the pack as a tool for building a positive partnership with parents. A meeting about the Ideas for Parents activities pack is likely to be well attended. The activities provide a practical focus that makes it is easy to introduce parents to ideas about learning in a straightforward, non-threatening manner.

Teachers can model the use of different activities in a hands-on manner, emphasising the need to avoid boring or forcing the children. They can encourage parents to see the ideas in the book as prompts for activities rather than as a set of demands – homework that must be carried out rigidly. They can discuss the importance of engaging children. They can demonstrate strategies for securing engagement e.g. by creating imaginary situations that provide reasons for solving a problem. They can discuss the need to let children take the initiative in deciding how an activity develops. They can emphasise how much everyone benefits when parents see the activities as opportunities for shared play, rather than setting out materials and leaving the child alone to get on with it.

By modelling and discussing developmentally appropriate play, practitioners can influence parents' ideas about teaching and learning; help them make well informed choices; and inspire the confidence to extend the activities provided and to come up with great new ideas of their own.

Overleaf we provide some examples of activities that are included in the *Ideas for Parents* activities pack.

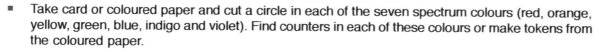

WHAT ELSE IS THE SAME COLOUR?

- Take card or coloured paper and cut a circle in each of the seven spectrum colours (red, orange, yellow, green, blue, indigo and violet). Find counters in each of these colours or make tokens from the coloured paper.

- Show the coloured circles to your child and invite them to focus on one colour at a time. Ask your child, "What else is the same colour as this circle?"

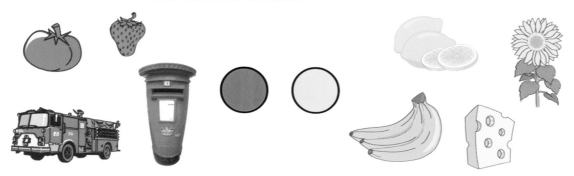

- Give your child a matching counter or token for each correctly named object. See how many objects s/he can name. Continue the game until all the colours have been used.

Key to Learning
Ideas for Parents

CATCH THE BALL

- You will need a large, a medium-sized and a small ball. Put the three balls on the floor. Look carefully at the balls, handle them and talk about them to your child. Use the size words to indicate which one is large, which one medium-sized and which one small.

- Put the balls in a row, arranged in order of size. Ask your child to give you the large ball. Put it back and ask for the medium-sized ball, then the small ball. Repeat the process, but this time ask for the small ball first, then the medium-sized ball then the large ball. Mix up the balls and ask your child to arrange them by size independently.

- Play "Which Size Catch". Tell your child to hold his/her arms wide apart to catch the large ball, closer together to catch the medium-sized ball and very close together to catch the small ball. Name a size, wait for your child to put his/her arms in the right position, then throw the appropriate ball. Alternatively, have your child ask you to throw a specific size of ball either verbally (naming a size) or by the position of his/her arms.

Key to Learning
Ideas for Parents

AND THEN WHAT WILL HAPPEN?

- Help your child to understand the consequences of everyday transformations. Talk about what happens next, e.g. what will happen if we do not put away our toys? If we do not put away our toys and we get out more toys then there will be no room on the carpet to walk. If there is no room to walk then people will walk on the toys. If people walk on the toys, the toys will get broken. Then there will be nothing to play with and we will feel sad, etc.

- As far as possible, create the chain of events by asking "And then what will happen?" If the consequences are undesirable, then the end point will naturally be sad feelings. If the consequences are desirable, e.g. if we decide to transform flour, fat, sugar, and milk into biscuits, then the end point will naturally be happy feelings. Where appropriate, help your child understand the difference between desirable and less desirable transformations!

Key to Learning
Ideas for Parents

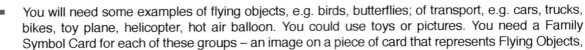

FAMILY SORT: TRANSPORT, FLYING OBJECTS AND AIR TRANSPORT

- You will need some examples of flying objects, e.g. birds, butterflies; of transport, e.g. cars, trucks, bikes, toy plane, helicopter, hot air balloon. You could use toys or pictures. You need a Family Symbol Card for each of these groups – an image on a piece of card that represents Flying Objects, another to represent Transport and one more to represent Air Transport. You also need to draw two large overlapping circles on a large piece of paper (Venn Diagram).

- Play "Family Sort". Put the Flying Objects symbol next to one circle, the Transport symbol next to the other and the Air Transport symbol next to the overlap. Help your child sort the objects into the correct Family Circles. Some objects belong to **both** families. Show your child how to solve the problem by "putting this one where the two families overlap".

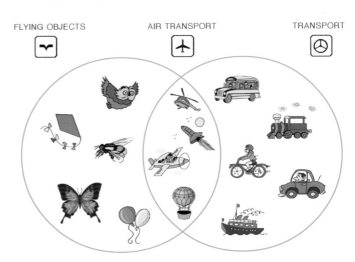

Key to Learning
Ideas for Parents

WHAT IS TALLER?

- Name five pieces of furniture in different rooms so your child cannot see them all at the same time! Ask him/her to guess the order of their height, i.e. to sequence them by height.

- Write down your child's guess. With the help of your child, measure the height of each piece of furniture. To do this, cut a piece of string or paper the same height as each piece of furniture; label the lengths so you do not forget which is which!

- When you have measured all the pieces, place the strips in sequence – longest to shortest. Check together to see if your child guessed correctly.

Key to Learning
Ideas for Parents

AS MANY CLAPS AS...

- Stamp your foot once and ask your child to "*make as many claps as there were stamps.*"

- Repeat for different numbers of stamps with different actions, e.g. winks, clicking fingers, clicks of the tongue.

- With young children it is very important to keep the number of claps low (no more than five at first, then up to as many as seven!).

- Swap roles so that your child asks you to "*make as many claps as there were stamps.*" Encourage your child to match your claps with actions to check whether the stamps match the claps.

- Make mistakes. When you do make a deliberate mistake stick to one clap too few or one clap too many.

- Remember that a young child who has thoroughly understood the meaning of *three claps, one clap too many* and *one clap too few* is far better off than one who can count to a hundred parrot fashion!

Key to Learning
Ideas for Parents

PICTURE CLUES

- Look together with your child at the story illustrations of "Goldilocks and the Three Bears" and talk about them.

- Play 'Picture Clues'. Tell your child you are going to give him/her clues about one of the illustrations and s/he has to guess which one it is as quickly as possible.

- Begin with more general clues, i.e. clues describing peripheral details: time of the year, nature, colours, objects, clothes, etc. Gradually make the clues more and more specific to the episode, by talking about the characters and their actions, until your child is able to guess correctly.

- Reverse roles. Ask your child to give clues about his/her favourite picture. Guess which one your child is describing.

Key to Learning
Ideas for Parents

PLAY "GUESS WHO I AM!"

- Mime one of the characters in the story of "Goldilocks and the Three Bears" and ask, "Guess who I am!"

- Exchange roles; let your child choose a character and perform a mime while you guess who it is.

- Involve as many family members as you can. The person who guesses correctly mimes the next character for the others to guess.

- Ask your child to close his/her eyes; imitate the speech of a character and ask your child to guess who is speaking. Exchange roles.

Key to Learning
Ideas for Parents

FUTURESCOPE

- Make a "Futurescope'. Cut out a circle in a piece of transparent paper (an overhead transparency or some other transparent material).

- Glue a thick card ring round the edges to make the Futurescope stronger and easier to hold.

- Look at different things through the Futurescope and guess how they will change, e.g. snow will turn into water, leaf buds into leaves, a baby into a child, etc.

Key to Learning
Ideas for Parents

CLAP – STAMP

- The aim of the game is to perform a sequence of actions represented by a pattern of shapes on a card.

- Show your child a drawing of a square. Tell your child that a square means clap your hands. Show your child a drawing of a circle. Tell your child that a circle means stamp your feet. Practice both actions.

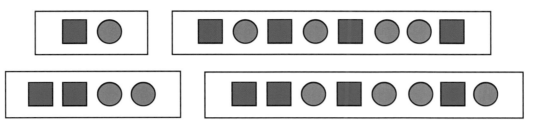

- Then show your child a card with two squares and two circles. When they can successfully follow the sequence (clap twice and stamp twice), try showing a series of cards with increasingly long and complex patterns.

- If your child finds it hard to manage independently, stamp and clap together.

Key to Learning
Ideas for Parents

FLOWER PETALS

- When you are out and about with your child look at flower petals that have been scattered by the wind, e.g. spring blossom.

- You will need green paper, different colours of paint, a thin brush and water to clean the brush.

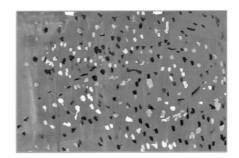

- Give your child a sheet of green paper and ask him/her to paint flower petals (short straight lines or small blobs) in different colours all over the lawn.

- Paint together, unless your child knows what to do and prefers you just to watch.

Key to Learning
Ideas for Parents

MOON AND STARS

- Spend time admiring the night sky with your child and discussing what you see. Then help him/her to paint a picture of it.

- You will need a piece of dark blue, dark grey or dark purple paper; yellow and orange paint; and two brushes (one thin and one thick).

- Now help your child to paint the moon and stars using yellow and orange paint to fill the sky with stars in a variety of sizes, colours and shades.

- Paint together, unless your child knows what to do and prefers you just to watch.

Key to Learning
Ideas for Parents

FIND THE TOY

- Draw a plan of a room together and then ask your child to leave the room or use a blindfold.

- Hide an object in the room (a toy, raisins or some similar treat). Use a counter to mark the position of the object on the plan. Then ask your child to come back into the room (or remove their blindfold).

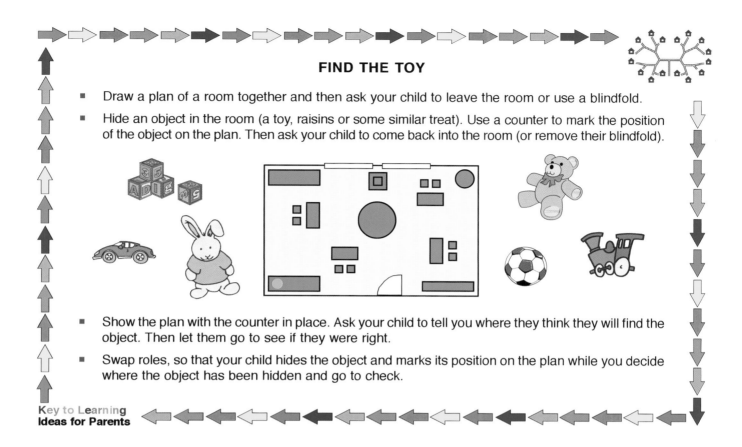

- Show the plan with the counter in place. Ask your child to tell you where they think they will find the object. Then let them go to see if they were right.

- Swap roles, so that your child hides the object and marks its position on the plan while you decide where the object has been hidden and go to check.

Key to Learning
Ideas for Parents

COMING HOME

- Help your child understand and use the preposition **behind**. You will need a few toy animals, each one smaller than the next (e.g. bear, fox, rabbit, hedgehog) and something to represent home (a bit of cloth, a box, a corner of the table).

- Tell your child that the animals have been playing in the forest, and now they have to go home to eat. Bear goes first, **behind** bear goes fox, **behind** fox goes rabbit, and **behind** rabbit goes hedgehog. Ask your child to help the animals go home in the right order.

- Next ask your child to help the animals go out to play again in the correct order (bear first, behind bear fox, behind fox rabbit, behind rabbit hedgehog).

- Encourage your child to use the preposition **behind** by emphasising the word yourself, and praising your child for using it. Use two, three or four animals to make the game easier or more difficult.

Key to Learning
Ideas for Parents

ROCKING DOLLS

- Inspire a love of language. Look at everyday objects and talk about them, using a rich vocabulary. Name objects and actions, use adjectives and adverbs to describe things vividly. Introduce synonyms (different words for the same thing) to convey subtle shades of meaning and opposites (antonyms) to help distinguish one thing from another.

- Introduce your child to a rich variety of traditional songs, poems and stories.

- Play increasingly complex sorting games with shapes of different sizes and colours.

- Make a collage of a Rocking Doll together. Ask your child to choose a coloured paper for the doll's dress. Cut out circles in three different sizes – a big circle for the body, a smaller circle for the head and two even smaller circles for the arms. Use more paper shapes (tiny circles, triangles, crescents) to add detail (eyes, hair, and mouth).

- Create the composition together, using praise, talk and your own enthusiasm to help maintain your child's interest and engagement. Encourage your child to work independently and talk about what s/he is doing.

- Celebrate the finished product. Find a place to display your child's Rocking Doll.

**Key to Learning
Ideas for Parents**

SPRING BLOSSOM

- Help your child to notice seasonal changes and common natural processes. Talk about the weather. Make connections between the weather and its most obvious consequences – we don't wear heavy winter clothing in spring, we will feel hot and sticky; we don't wear light summery clothes in winter we will feel cold; we may still need to wear cardigans and jackets in spring. Draw your child's attention to the fact that most trees have no leaves at the beginning of the year. Watch as the buds begin to swell and grow. Notice that there are differences between trees; some flower before the leaves open, some open their leaves first.

- This activity works particularly well in spring. Make a tree with no leaves. Explain what you are doing as you create the basic shape, using strips of paper or tissue in a variety of lengths and thicknesses for the trunk, branches and twigs. Ask your child to help you add blossom to show that spring has arrived. Use scraps of rumpled paper for the blossom, creating a 3D effect.

- This is an ideal technique for engaging a small child as most of them will take great pleasure in actually crumpling the paper, before sticking "the spring blossom" to the tree. Display the finished tree.

**Key to Learning
Ideas for Parents**

COPYCAT

- Take any two pairs of identical building blocks. Keep one pair yourself and give the other pair to your child. Build different structures with the two blocks very slowly so that your child can see exactly what you are doing. Ask your child to copy your actions.

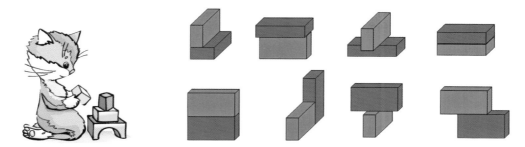

- Now build a different structure more quickly, asking your child to copy you exactly. Then change roles.

- Finally challenge him/her to build as many different structures as possible.

Key to Learning
Ideas for Parents

KEEP ME IN – KEEP ME OUT

- Talk to your child about fences; discuss the fact that there are many different types of fence because fences are used for many different purposes.

- Talk about what makes particular fences suitable for the job they do (a low fence around a flowerbed lets us see the pretty flowers and reminds us not to walk on them; a high fence around animals in the zoo keeps them safely inside their space).

- Give your child a variety of toy animals and ask him/her to build fences "to keep the animals and their visitors safe."

Key to Learning
Ideas for Parents

WHERE DOES THE WIND COME FROM?

- Many children believe that the swaying of trees causes the wind. Do not argue with them about this. Instead, wrap up warmly and go for walks together on windy days. Look at what you can see and talk about it. Make opportunities to point out that it isn't just the branches of the trees that are moving. Everything that can move does move: flags and clothes on the washing line flap, rubbish swirls, autumn leaves rustle, doors slam, clouds scud across the sky. Just like all the rest of the movement we can see around us on windy days, the swaying of branches is caused by the wind. The movement we see is an effect and not a cause.

- If possible, take your child to a place that has both swaying trees and a space without trees. Look at the branches swaying in the wind, and agree that the wind is blowing. Look at the place where there are no trees and ask the child to guess whether or not the wind will also be blowing there. Move into the treeless space and find out. With time, repeated observation and talk, your child should come to see for him/herself that swaying branches are one of the effects of the wind, rather than its cause.

Key to Learning
Ideas for Parents

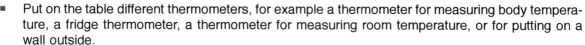

THERMOMETER

- Put on the table different thermometers, for example a thermometer for measuring body temperature, a fridge thermometer, a thermometer for measuring room temperature, or for putting on a wall outside.

- Use the thermometer to track changes of temperature between night and day – the temperature rises if it gets warmer, falls if it gets colder.

- Talk about changes in water temperature when you make a hot drink. The water in the kettle starts off cold and becomes hot. Then we pour the hot water into a teapot or a cup and the water cools – first the water was too hot to drink, then it cools enough for us to drink, but if we leave the drink too long it becomes cold.

- Similarly, talk about changes in the temperature of cooked food.

Key to Learning
Ideas for Parents

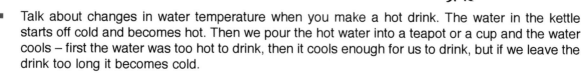

YES – NO

- You will need a hand puppet with a moveable head. It will answer simple "yes" or "no" questions by nodding or shaking its head.

- Ask the puppet simple questions, e.g. "Do you like football?"

- Each time the hand puppet answers a question, check that your child understands the meaning of the puppet's response: "What did it say? Did it say 'Yes'? Did it nod its head? Did it say 'No'? Did it shake its head?"

- For a more complicated version of the game ask your child to answer simple yes/no questions using only gestures – a nod for "yes", and a shake of the head for "no". No words allowed!

- Change roles and let your child ask the questions. Make mistakes and let them catch you out.

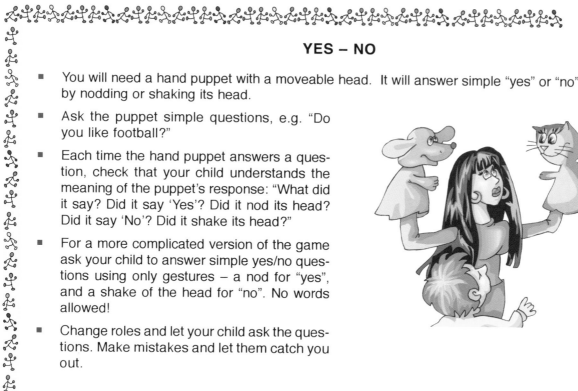

Key to Learning
Ideas for Parents

SMALL AS A BALL AND GROW TALL

- When you are at home or out and about with your child the following games are helpful in understanding size and the concept of transformation.

- Play "Watch Me Grow." Say, "Show me what you were like when you were very small." Get your child to crouch down into a tiny ball. Then get them to say "Watch me grow!" while they straighten up to end on tiptoes. Then stretch your arms up as high as possible to show what they will be like when they have grown even more. Get them to copy your actions.

- Play "Big Steps, Small Steps." Say, "Now show me how you used to walk when you were very small." Get your child to walk with small steps.

- Say, "Now show me how you will walk when you get very big!" Get your child to grow as in the first game and then walk taking big strides with arms swinging.

- Now say "Small again!", then "Big again". The game can continue until your child is ready to stop or you have run out of time or energy.

- It can help to use a musical instrument to mark big and small steps, for example. high-pitched sounds (chime bars, triangle) for small steps, low pitched notes (drum) for large steps.

Key to Learning
Ideas for Parents

ALIVE OR NOT ALIVE?

- Cut out at least 20 pictures from magazines and newspapers. Make sure you have a mix of non-living objects, animals and plants. Spread all the pictures on the floor.

- Ask your child to split the pictures into **two** separate families. If necessary, help him/her to understand that the most appropriate families are living things (animate) and non-living things (inanimate).

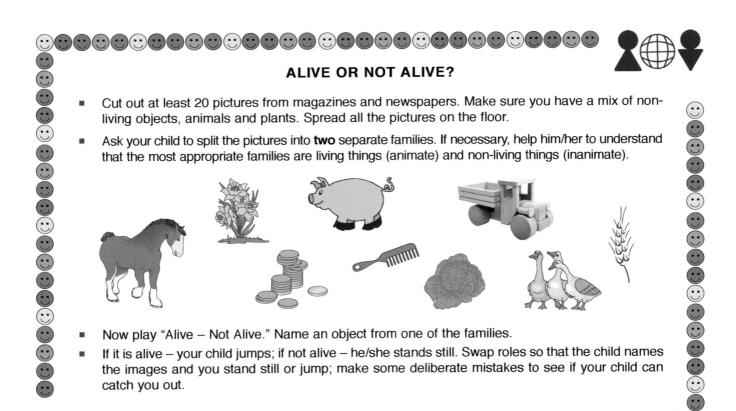

- Now play "Alive – Not Alive." Name an object from one of the families.

- If it is alive – your child jumps; if not alive – he/she stands still. Swap roles so that the child names the images and you stand still or jump; make some deliberate mistakes to see if your child can catch you out.

Key to Learning
Ideas for Parents

MY MORNING

- Help your child learn to interpret ("read") a sequence of symbols. Talk to him/her about your normal morning routine.

- Make simple drawings of routine morning activities on pieces of card: waking up, washing, cleaning teeth, brushing hair, getting dressed and eating breakfast.

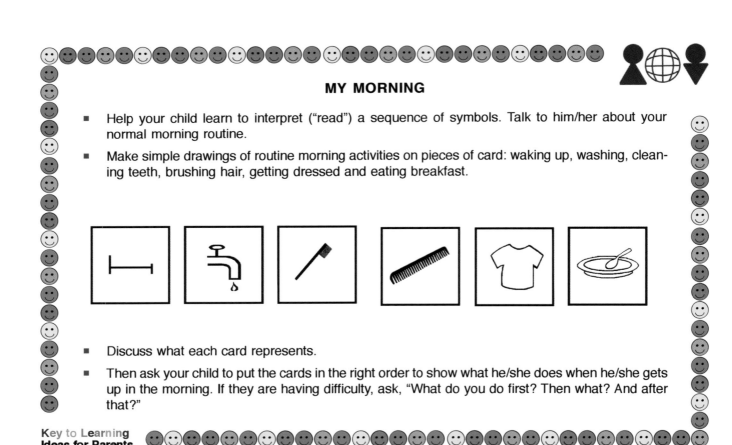

- Discuss what each card represents.

- Then ask your child to put the cards in the right order to show what he/she does when he/she gets up in the morning. If they are having difficulty, ask, "What do you do first? Then what? And after that?"

Key to Learning
Ideas for Parents

WHAT PEOPLE SAY ...

Came – Saw – Listened – Loved it!
Hope we have the courage.
Viva butterflies!

Sue Palmer

- PROFESSIONAL OPINIONS

- WHAT PARENTS SAY...

PROFESSIONAL OPINIONS

■ Key to Learning is phenomenally impressive. It has depth and breadth, rigour and flexibility, insight and inclusion. It truly is a Vygotskian approach, carrying through to the 21st Century his monumental discovery that human learning and development are a unified whole. Unlike any other curriculum I am aware of, "Key to Learning" relates to young children as, in Vygotsky's words, "a head taller than they are" – which is an essential characteristic of a developmental learning environment.

Lois Holzman,author of "Lev Vygotsky: Revolutionary Scientist"

■ One of my research officers visited one of your private nurseries and was just bowled over by the work the children were doing. She thinks your programme is brilliant! And so do I.

Professor Kathy Sylva, Oxford University

■ My mind is still buzzing with the ideas you sparked. If only the whole of the British preschool education could have taken on Vygotskian principles, there would have been no need to write our gloomy report.

Claire Mills, Producer of "Too Much Too Young" Channel 4 Dispatches

■ I am sure that this initiative has implications for the nation as a whole. I have seen preschools all over the world. There are some excellent examples, particularly in New Zealand, USA and Northern Italy, but this one is outstanding. I do not believe I have seen a better one the world over.

Sir Christopher Ball, Chancellor of the University of Derby
Co-author of Start Right Report "The Importance of Early Learning"

■ What sets Key to Learning apart from any other preschool that I have ever seen is the depth of conceptual planning that has gone into the school. It literally sparkles with superb original educational ideas. The emphasis at the school is on the development of children's abilities to think in symbolic terms – leading to higher order thinking skills in later life.

Colin Rose, Accelerated Learning Systems

■ As a literacy specialist who has spent the last few years working in Early Years, I was deeply impressed. The levels of language and cognitive skills displayed by the children were remarkable, and the activities were imaginative and exciting. In an environment rich with opportunities for child-initiated learning, all children also had two daily small-group sessions, carefully structured to develop a wide range of skills and learning styles.

Sue Palmer, Times Educational Supplement

■ The whole Key to Learning Curriculum ties in well with the government recommendations and focuses on the development of the early language and communication skills.

I believe that with the programme we may well be on the way to creating a "level playing field" for children when they start full-time education in areas where there are high levels of social deprivation. In addition, the programme is designed for all the children, regardless of ability and the evidence suggests that it is also beneficial for the most able. In conclusion, Key to Learning is a scheme that will enhance the developing skills of young children. I fully endorse its philosophy and recommend that we extend the number of participating pupils by encouraging more schools in the County to adopt it as part of their early-years curriculum.

Dr Madeleine Portwood, Specialist Senior Educational Psychologist,
Durham Local Education Authority

■ Key to Learning has some super ideas. I like the way the children are not threatened in any way by language initially. They have this lovely confidence in telling stories so that when they get to year one, they are ready to take off and start reading and writing.

Nanette Paine, Headteacher, Two Waters Primary School

■ We have been using the Key to Learning educational programme in the Foundation Stage at William Reynolds Infant School since September 2005. The program has made a tremendous difference to the engagement of all pupils in their work and offers them the best start to their educational life. Children are able to develop the learning abilities and think creatively through planning and communication. There is evidence that pupils have higher levels of linguistic engagement. The principles of Vygotsky remain embedded in the lively, exciting programme that fits well into Excellence and Enjoyment: A Strategy for Primary Schools where it states that: "The goal is for every primary school to combine excellence in teaching with enjoyment of learning".

Meg Thompson, Headteacher, William Reynolds Infant School

■ The process of learning starts when a baby comes into the world and continues during life. This process of learning and development is based upon a dialogue between the child and the environment. During this process, tools and skills are developed in order to fulfil needs and solve problems the child faces. Sometimes this process of learning is random – life supplies the need for learning. On these occasions, there is an option to develop the skills needed for learning, but we cannot be certain that all the concepts and skills that a child needs for a high level of thinking and learning are developed. Therefore developing a structural learning process, which is determined by the culture, and the goals that are set by it, is necessary for the development of a child.

Key to Learning is a curriculum that builds tools systematically. These basic tools -concepts and skills, which are a foundation for the development of high levels of thinking and learning – are presented in a clear and precise way through the materials. This creates the opportunity for a child to work with them and build the skills and knowledge required. While working through the problems the programme presents, the children learn how to deal with the task and to develop the strategy needed to solve the problem, as well as use the correct concepts needed for it.

The structure of the programme helps to generalise a concept by using it in different contexts and different modalities. It also offers opportunities for repetition, which helps to crystallise experiences into concepts and skills. Using these concepts and skills in different situations and activities helps the child to internalise them so they become part of the child's repertoire.

The learning process within the programme is well structured, built on clearly defined steps, and using a range of modalities, which helps to internalise the targeted concept. The development of these strategies helps the child to develop literacy and numeracy skills as well as becoming well equipped for learning within a classroom setting.

Dr Ruth Kaufmann, University of Tel Aviv, Israel

■ All of the ex-pupils who were followed up in their new educational placement had settled in well and seemed to be achieving at the top of the ability range in the class. Without exception, all the teachers of the children followed up spoke of the children's positive attitudes to learning, their excellent relationships with adults and peers, their ability to work independently, their articulateness and willingness to contribute to discussion, and their ability to make choices and state preferences. It seemed, thus, as though they had been very well prepared for school and, with regard to the older pupils, had maintained their excellent start.

National Foundation for Educational Research (NFER)
Interim Evaluation Report 2000

■ In my forty years of research in education, I have never seen a programme that develops language and communication as effectively as 'Key to Learning' does. Observation in the settings suggested that the impact of this programme was greatest on the child's vocabulary, creative language and focussed attention. This was confirmed by experimental data which was collected at three time points and involved 83 children (aged 3 and 4). There were significant differences in the children's vocabulary and creative language. One group made on average 20 months progress during the 12 months of the intervention. Some children advanced three years. A second group on average made 18 months progress after 7 months of intervention. Clearly "Key to Learning" has a marked impact on the child's cognitive development and language skills.

Dr Madeleine Portwood, Specialist Senior Educational Psychologist,
Durham Local Education Authority

■ As an educational psychologist working within North Ayrshire Council I was delighted to be involved in carrying out a pilot study of Developmental Games one of the components in the Key To Learning curriculum. The programme matched closely with the existing Scottish curriculum and was used with preschool, primary and special school pupils. One of the most interesting findings in the qualitative data from the study was the diversity of impact of the programme on children's learning and manifestation of this. Although the main emphasis is upon visual and spatial skills and creativity, staff reports indicate significant impact upon, language and communication, co-operation and confidence. I look forward to an ongoing involvement with this exciting curricular programme.

Shonah McKechnie, Senior Educational Psychologist,
North Ayrshire Council, Scotland

■ I am astounded by the children's ability to work together to retell traditional stories. Story Grammar dramatically enhances children's understanding of stories and their ability to retell stories. The use of language is outstanding,

Tracey Wilson, Headteacher of Lumley Nursery and Infant School,
Durham Local Education Authority

■ The Chelsea Group of Children is the first school in England to use Key to Learning in teaching children with developmental challenges. The Program not only improved cognitive functions across the spectrum but also enabled teachers to spot specific areas of difficulties in a child's abilities and understanding. We feel this approach should be used in all nursery schools and especially for children with special needs. Within the popular movements in education, one essential component has been missing and that is practical application in the classroom. Galina Dolya has developed learning activities and materials, based on Vygotsky's Theory of Education, and accompanied by clear and comprehensive instructions which can be immediately incorporated into the early year's curriculum. Our student's responses to the programme have obliged us to document our experience of the process and the results so other educators may benefit.

We at Chelsea Group have delved into the best, research based practices in education available in Europe and the United States and we have found Key to Learning offers the most comprehensive and effective, yet simplest program we have used over the past 10 years.

Libby Hartman, Director of the Chelsea Group of Children, Developmental
Assessment and Diagnostic Teaching Centre, London

■ The Foundation Stage Profile (total) scores have increased from 67.0 in 2005 to 81.1 in 2006. Personal, Social and Emotional Development, Knowledge and Understanding of the World, Physical Development and Creative Development have increased significantly. Moderation exercises undertaken by staff show that assessment procedures are very good. (Ref: Moderation Report)

This is as a result of the investment in the Key to Learning Programme which is followed within the Foundation Stage. The Vygotsky approach to learning extends children's ability to think and communicate by using mental tools in a systematic way. (Ref. "The Key to Learning Programme").

The Foundation Stage staff have become pioneers for this way of learning and have been involved in the training and development of other teachers.

Extract from report of Headteacher of William Reynolds Infant School to OFSTED

■ William Reynolds Infant School is a good school with an outstanding curriculum which underpins pupils' outstanding personal development and good achievement.

Children come into the Nursery with low standards; the skills associated with communication and social skills are particularly weak. Teachers work very hard to ensure that children make good progress in developing their speaking and listening skills and outstanding strides in their personal development. This provides a firm foundation for their work in Years 1 and 2.

Many pupils start school unable to manage their own actions but the school works very hard to improve pupils' conduct and this results in outstanding standards of behaviour.

The curriculum in the Nursery and Reception classes has been recently improved and now meets the pupils' needs very well.

Pupils start the Nursery class with low standards. They make good progress through the Nursery and Reception classes because of good teaching and a very well structured curriculum.

Pupils' spiritual, moral, social and cultural development is outstanding. Children's personal development in the Nursery and Reception classes is excellent because of the strong focus on helping children to act sensibly and to share with others.

However, the creative elements of the curriculum are also well addressed and this adds to pupils' enjoyment of school.

Extracts from Ofsted Report 2007

■ As a long standing theoretician and pragmatist of pre-school education I was convinced, that there was nothing else for me to discover in this domain, that I had already achieved everything in my professional career and I was ready to retire.

 However, working with "Key to Learning" has changed the routine and taken away the professional burn-out. It gave me the impetus and desire for further research and it made me sure that now I cannot walk away I have so much more to do."

Anna Natora, *Headteacher of Nursery School 14,*
Masovia, Poland

■ The program "Key to Learning" has a form of systematic, logical integrity which is constructed from thematically coherent sessions and modules. It enables teachers to accomplish definite objectives by taking into consideration the idea of a "step by step" developmental curriculum. Therefore it has the unusual advantage to follow the individual development of the individual.

The programme prepares the child to manage situations in their lives by developing key abilities, such as self-regulation, concentration and abstract thinking. It also develops the language and communication competences of a child which form the foundation of his relationships with peers and adults. Opportunities for group activities that appear in many sessions promote to the child a challenge to work to the maximum of ability. Thanks to this, his self-esteem and position in peer group is strengthened.

With "Key to learning" the child evolves gradually and systematically from the stage of "caterpillar" into a "butterfly" - to a maturity to enable him to function effectively in school environment. We feel huge satisfaction when we are looking at the programme from the trainers' perspective and it has changed our life dramatically. Thanks to "Key" and Galina's personal input we have discovered copious creativeness and we have also become more "open". We have learnt how to effectively use the time to fulfill new tasks and personal dreams.

Dorota Kamińska and Bożena Świderska, *Consultants of MSCDN,*
Warsaw, Poland

■ I attended your course in North Lanarkshire, Scotland earlier this year. I was inspired by the concepts behind the "Key to Learning" and the wonderful activities in the books.

When the children, Primary One (4 to 5 year olds) commenced in August 2006, I introduced the 4 programmes to them. The children responded with great enthusiasm and their level of engagement has been such as I have not witnessed before. This cohort had been flagged up from their nursery as having a number of children with a range of social and academic difficulties.

As the sessions have progressed, I have begun to observe how quickly this group can absorb new learning across all curricular areas. Moreover the problems that were indicated by the nursery staff have not arisen.

I have taught Primary One children many times and I can honestly report that the Key to Learning has improved the child's acquisition of new skills and given me great pleasure working with children who are displaying such a thirst for learning.

Monika Dick, *Kilsyth Primary, North Lanarkshire, Scotland*

■ A huge thank you. I am very excited at the prospect of following up today's journey into the magic kingdom for the quest to find the Key to Learning.

Sharon Lamont, *Millburn Primary School, Northern Ireland*

■ Excellent practical ideas with underpinning knowledge and pedagogy, a most inspiring and excellent programme. Key to Learning really opens those windows of opportunity for children "the key to the future".

Una Gossey, *Early Years Advisory Officer, County Antrim, Northern Ireland*

■ I knew where I wanted to go
I knew what I wanted to give children
I didn't know where to go for the answers
I stood still

I was afraid of falling
You gave me wings and a way to go
Now I know I can go to the edge
I know we can fly

Sarah Sissons, *Headteacher, Somercotes Infant School, Derbyshire*

NORTH AYRSHIRE EVALUATION OF DEVELOPMENTAL GAMES PROGRAMME

WHAT DID THE TEACHERS SAY ABOUT ...

THEIR VIEW OF CHILDREN'S LEARNING

■ "It has been an eye opener in highlighting what the children are actually thinking."

■ "I think I have undermined their learning in the past. They are capable of more than I give them credit for."

■ "It's made me aware that children learn in very different ways."

WHERE IT FITS IN THEIR CURRICULUM

■ "It fits into every area particularly knowledge and understanding."

■ "It fits in well especially expressive and aesthetic and thinking skills."

■ "Some activities showed themselves up as a gap that I felt the curriculum didn't provide for the children."

HOW IT COMPARES WITH OTHER LESSONS

- "With Key to Learning there's more opportunity for interaction...and for the children to think about their ideas."
- "There was more than one answer as long as they could justify their ideas."
- "The games brought more out in the children like thinking, talking and co-operating with each other."

THE CHILDREN'S REACTIONS

- "One girl would not speak at the start of term but then she realised her answers were as good as everyone else's and she really came out of herself"
- "One boy has really improved in confidence, he's so quick at seeing things – I probably wouldn't have found that out about him without Key to Learning."

THE DIFFERENCES IN THE CHILDREN

- "Their ability to work co-operatively has improved – I would say above levels of what I would normally expect from children at this stage of Primary One."
- "The quieter ones speak out more and the louder ones have learnt to wait their turn and let others contribute their ideas."

DEVELOPING "DEVELOPMENTAL GAMES"

- "It seems to be a forerunner for Formative Assessment Strategies. It opens up levels of communication, raises self-esteem and focuses children on learning strategies and approaches."

Shonah McKechnie, *North Ayrshire Psychological Services, Scotland*

WHAT PARENTS SAY...

- Dear Galina, I wanted to write and let you know how well Alice is doing after attending the Key to Learning sessions.

The move to Cornwall has been difficult at times for Alice. We enrolled her to the local all girl prep school. She settled quickly and went on to win a partial scholarship that begins in September. **Alice took part in a national maths test, and was one of only two girls to achieve the Gold level in**

This is Alice, age 3, in 1994. She followed the full Key to Learning Curriculum and then stayed in the Saturday Enrichment programme for a further five years.

her school. Alice enjoys Maths, English and Art, and is looking forward to Latin classes in the next year or so. She has taken Speech and Drama classes and performed well in local events, coming amongst the top contenders. She also won a Harry Potter competition, and was one of twenty children nationally to spend a weekend at Hogwarts – a terrific prize.

Well I hope you have enjoyed this update on Alice's progress, I know if I were you I would be wondering what has happened to all the children you have been involved with. Alice continues to delight and surprise us with her creativity and ability to understand complex ideas. Thank you for all your input and I will endeavour to write again with her progress.

*Best wishes, **Emma Helliwell***

■ Parents have observed significant improvements with their children described as being more thoughtful, analytical, interested, engaged with their environment, able to concentrate and enthused, because of the Key to Learning programme.

Independent research consultants

■ Dear Galina, just a few lines to tell you how much we think Alexander benefited from his attendance at the Key to Learning pre-school sessions. Looking back there is little doubt that in comparison to his peers at school, he exhibited superior reading, logic and number skills, and also his powers of concentration were notable. His confidence and self-esteem were helped considerably by the pre-school sessions and his language and communication abilities were further markedly advanced. We are so glad that Alexander was able to take advantage of what Key to Learning had to offer, and provide him with a fantastic basis to his academic career and life generally.

***Theo Theodosiou**,*
parent of a child that is now at key stage 4

"Come to the edge."
        "We can't we are afraid."
"Come to the edge."
        "We can't we will fall."
"Come to the edge."
        And they came.
And he pushed them…
        And they flew.

                Apollinaire

How does one become a butterfly?
You must want to fly so much
that you are willing to give up
being a caterpillar.

Paulos

THE BEGINNING ...

REFERENCES

■ **Arievitch, I. & Stetsenko, A.** (2000) The quality of cultural tools and cognitive development: Galperin's perspective and its implications. *Human Development*, 43.

■ **Arievitch, I. & Stetsenko, A.** (2002) Teaching, learning and development: a post-Vygotskian perspective. In G. Wells & G. Claxton (Eds.) *Learning in the life of the 21ˢᵗ century: Sociocultural perspectives on the future of education*). Malden, MA: Blackwell.

■ **Bodrova, E. & Leong, D.** (1996) *Tools of the mind*. Englewood Cliffs, N.J: Prentice Hall.

■ **Daniels, H., Cole, M. & Wertch, J.** (Eds.) (2007) *The Cambridge Companion to Vygotsky*. New York: Cambridge University Press.

■ **Davydov, V. V.** (1996) Teoriya razvivayuschego obucheniya [The theory of developmental teaching]. Moscow: INTOR.

■ **Dyachenko, O.M.** (Ed.) (1995) *Pedagogicheskaya diagnostika po programme Razvitie* [Pedagogical diagnostics in programme Development]. Moscow: Venger Centre.

■ **Dyachenko, O.M.** (Ed.) (1995) *Programma Odarionnyi Rebionok* [Programme Gifted Child]. Moscow: Novaya Shkola.

■ **Dyachenko, O.M.** (Ed.) (1996) *Razvitie voobrazheniya doshkolnika* [The development of imagination in preschool children]. Moscow: PIRAO.

■ **Dyachenko, O. M.** (Ed.) (1997). *Odarionny rebionok* [Gifted child] Moscow: MOPK.

■ **Dyachenko, O.M.** (Ed.) (2000) *Razvitie: programma novogo pokolieniya dlya doshkolnyh obrazovatelnyh uchrezhdeniy* [Development: New generation programme for educating preschoolers]. Moscow: GNOM.

■ **Dyachenko, O. M., & Veraksa, N. E.** (1990) *Tochka, tochka, dva krjuchochka* [Dot, dot, two hooks – smiley face]. Moscow: Pedagogika.

■ **Dyachenko, O. M. & Veraksa, N. E.** (1994) *Chego na svietie nie byvayet?* [And pigs might fly!]. Moscow: Znanie.

■ **Elkonin, D.** (1978) *Psikhologiya igry* [The psychology of play]. Moscow: Pedagogika.

■ **Gardner, H.** (1984) Frames of Mind. Great Britain: Heinemann.

■ **Karpov, Y. V.** (2005) *The neo-Vygotskian approach to child development*. New York: Cambridge University Press.

■ **Kozulin, A.** (1990) *Vygotsky's psychology: a biography of ideas*. Cambridge, MA: Harvard University Press.

■ **Kozulin, A.** (1998) *Psychological tools: a socio-cultural approach to education*. Cambridge, MA: Harvard University Press.

■ **Kozulin, A., Gindis, B., Ageyev, V., Miller, S.** (Eds.) (2003) *Vygotsky's educational theory in cultural context*. New York: Cambridge University Press.

■ **Leont'ev, A.N.** (1981). *Problems in the development of the mind*. Moscow: Progress Publishers.

■ **Luria, A. R.** (1976) *Cognitive development: Its cultural and social foundations*. Cambridge, MA: Harvard University Press.

■ **Luria, A. R.** (1995) Razvitie konstructivnoi deyatilnosti doshkolnika [The development of constructive abilities in preschool children] in *A. Leon'tev and A. Zaporozhets (Eds.) Voprosy psikhologii rebionka doshkologo vosrasta*. Moscow: MOPK.

■ **Mihailenko, N. Y. & Korotkova, N.A.** (2002) *Igra s pravilami v doshkolnom vosraste* [Playing games with rules in preschool age]. Moscow: Akademicheskii Proekt.

■ **Newman, F. & Holzman, L.** (2002) *Lev Vygotsky: revolutionary scientist*. New York: Routledge.

■ **Obukhova, L.** (1996) *Detskaya psychologiya* [Child psychology]. Moscow: Rospedagenstvo.

■ **Venger. L. A.** (1977) *The emergence of perceptual actions*. In M. Cole (Ed.) Soviet Developmental Psychology: An Anthology. White Plains, NY: M. E. Sharpe.

■ **Venger, L. A.** (1978) *Nasha gruppa* [Our group]. Moscow: Znanie.

■ **Venger, L. A.** (Ed.) (1986) *Razvitie poznavatelnych sposobnostey v protsesse doshkolnogo vospitaniya* [Development of cognitive abilities in preschool education]. Moscow: Pedagogika.

■ **Venger, L. A.** (Ed.) (1988) *The origin and development of cognitive abilities in preschool children*. International Journal of Behavioural Development, 11(2).

■ **Venger, L. A.** (Ed.) (1994) *Programma Razvitie: Osnovniye polozheniya* [Programme Development: Main principles]. Moscow: Novaya Shkola.

■ **Venger, L. A.** (Ed.) (1996) *Slovo i obraz v reshenii poznavatelnykh zadach doshkolnikami* [Word and image in the preschoolers' cognitive problem solving]. Moscow: INTOR.

■ **Venger, L. A. & Dyachenko, O. M.** (Eds.) (1989) *Igry i uprazhneniya po razvitiyu umstvennych sposobnostei u detei doshkol'nogo vozrasta* [Games and activities developing cognitive abilities in preschool children]. Moscow: Prosvescheniye.

■ **Venger, L. A. & Kholmovskaya, V. V.** (Eds.) (1978) *Diagnostika umstvennogo razvitiya doshkolnikov* [Assessment of cognitive development of preschool children]. Moscow: Pedagogika.

■ **Venger, L. A., Martsinkovskaya, T. D. & Venger, A. L.** (1994) *Gotov li vash rebionok k shkole?* [Is you child ready for school?] Moscow: Znanie.

■ **Venger, L. A. & Venger, A. L.** (1994) *Domashniaya shkola* [Home-school]. Moscow: Znanie.

■ **Veraksa, N. E.** (Ed.) (2005) *Dialekticheskoye obucheniye* [Dialectical education]. Moscow: Eureka.

■ **Veraksa, N. E.** (Ed.) (2007) Diagnostika gotovnosti rebionka k shkolie [Diaganostics of child's readiness for school]. Moscow: Mozaika-Sintez.

■ **Veraksa, N. E. & Dyachenko, O. M.** (1991) *Yescho nie pozdno* [It's not too late]. Moscow: Znanie.

■ **Veraksa, N. E. & Dyachenko, O. M.** (2003) *Individualnie osobennosti poznavatielnogo razvitiya dietei doshkolnogo vozrasta* [Individual characteristics of cognitive development in preschool children]. Moscow: PERCE.

■ **Veraksa, N. E. & Veraksa A. N.** (2006) *Razvitie rebionka v doshkolnom detstvie* [Child's development in preschool age]. Moscow: Mozaika – Sintez.

■ **Veraksa, N. E. & Veraksa A. N.** (2006). *Zarubezhnie psichologi o razviti rebionka doshkolnika* [Western psychologists about development of preschool children]. Moscow: Mozaika-Sintez.

■ **Vygotsky, L. S.** (1978) *Mind in Society: The development of higher mental processes*. Cambridge, MA: Harvard University.

■ **Vygotsky, L. S.** (1986) *Thought and Language*. Cambridge, MA: MIT Press.

■ **Vygotsky, L. S.** (1998) *Child psychology*. New York: Plenum Press.

■ **Zaporozhets, A. V. & Elkonin, D. B.** (Eds.) (1971) *The psychology of preschool children*. Cambridge, MA: MIT Press.

■ **Zaporozhets, A. V. & Lisina, M. I.** (Eds.) (1974) *Razvitie obscheniya u doshkolnikov* [The development of communication in preschoolers]. Moscow: Pedagogika.

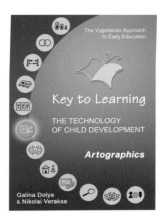

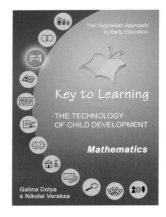

Galina Dolya, Butterfly House, 14 Mount Road, Wheathampstead, Herts. AL4 8BX

Tel. +44 (0) 1582 831360   E-mail: keytolearning@fsmail.net

www.keytolearning.com